Striving to Be Like Jesus

A Study of His Characteristics and How We Can Make Them Our Own

To this you were called,
because Christ suffered for you, leaving you an example,
that you should follow in his steps.
I Peter 2:21

David and Cynthia Lanius

MILLERSVILLE CHURCH OF CHRIST
1158 Louisville Highway
Goodlettsville, TN 37072
Phone: 615-859-1841
Website: www.millersvillechurch.com

Striving to Be Like Jesus: A Study of His Characteristics and How We Can Make Them Our Own

ISBN 979-8-9880304-0-9

Unless otherwise noted, scripture quotations are taken from the (NASB®) New American Standard Bible®, Copyright © 1995 by The Lockman Foundation. Used by permission. All rights reserved. www.lockman.org
Printed in the United States of America

Cover art https://shotstash.com/license/

MILLERSVILLE CHURCH OF CHRIST
1188 Louisville Highway
Goodlettsville, TN 37072
Phone. 615-859-1841
Website: www.millersvillechurch.com

DEDICATION

On June 30, 1966, we said to each other, "I take thee, to have and to hold from this day forward, according to God's holy ordinance, for better, for worse, for richer, for poorer, in sickness and in health, to love and to cherish, forsaking all others for as long as we both shall live." With these words, we became husband and wife.

For our lives together, we are grateful to God. For our hurts against the other, we are deeply sorry. For our joys shared, we delight. Our lesson to others is that you can weather the storms of life together if you are committed to God and to one another. We have proved that in marriage, as in all of life, God's way is the best way and to one another, we lovingly dedicate this book.

David and Cynthia Lanius

Marriage is honorable
Hebrews 13:4

CONTENTS

INTRODUCTION

"Everyone when he is fully trained will be like his teacher."
Luke 6:40b

Jesus is our perfect example. He lived exactly as God intended for all of us to live. "For you have been called for this purpose, since Christ also suffered for you, leaving you an example for you to follow in His steps" (1 Peter 2:21). How do we please God? We learn to live like Jesus. A familiar old hymn entitled, *Oh to be Like Thee,* says, "This is my constant longing and prayer." Consider the intensity of that effort! We may say we want to be like Jesus, but we will not wake up one morning and suddenly find ourselves like Him. To know Him and follow Him will take our life-long devotion.

How do we learn to walk as Jesus walked, to love as He loved, to devote our lives to God as He did? It must start within our hearts. We must want to *be* like Jesus, not just *do* like Him. If we have the heart of Jesus, we are the best we can be. Is that not what we want for our lives? Enough to make it our "constant longing and prayer?"

We should approach it with joy. On one hand, following Jesus is not a mission for the faint-hearted. Consider Matthew 16:24 where Jesus said to His disciples, "If anyone wishes to come after Me, he must deny himself, and take up his cross and follow Me." Self-denial can be a tremendous challenge, can it not? But we must trust God to provide us with what we need to accomplish it. Jesus also said that His yoke is easy and His burden is light (Matthew 11:30). Compared to the yoke of evil and the burden of sin, Jesus' yoke is light and easy. Since Jesus says it is easy, we must not make it hard and burdensome.

Since it is where we learn of Him, we cannot know Jesus without knowing His word. Consequently, this is a *Bible* study. Our

1

space is limited, and in this book, we want it to be *God's* words, not man's, that inspire us to become more like Jesus. Paul used this same approach with the Corinthians "so that [their] faith would not rest on the wisdom of men, but on the power of God" (1 Corinthians 2:5).

What abundant support we receive in our walk! What could be more encouraging than Hebrews 12:1-2? The writer says: "Therefore, since we have so great a cloud of witnesses surrounding us, let us also lay aside every encumbrance and the sin which so easily entangles us, and let us run with endurance the race that is set before us, ²fixing our eyes on Jesus, the author and perfecter of faith, who for the joy set before Him endured the cross, despising the shame, and has sat down at the right hand of the throne of God."

As we run our race, we are surrounded by that great cloud of witnesses, the faithful of all ages. They have finished the race, and their examples encourage us. Then we look to Jesus. He has finished it, too, perfectly. See Him at the finish line cheering us on, pleading tenderly when we need it, and supporting us when we are at our weakest. That is the Jesus that we strive to be like.

About this book: We describe 51 attributes and actions of Jesus and in each lesson encourage us to make them our own. We have arranged them in alphabetical order so that a topic will be easier to find. You may want to look through the list and go first to ones that seem more compelling, more helpful, or more needed. When we refer to "Vine's", we are referring to *Vine's Complete Expository Dictionary of Old and New Testament Words.* "Strong's" is *The Strong's Exhaustive Concordance.* We have also included hymns that inspire, almost exclusively old ones that we all know.

HYMN

O to Be Like Thee! T Chisholm (1897) Public Domain

O to be like Thee! Blessed Redeemer;
This is my constant longing and prayer;
Gladly I'll forfeit all of earth's treasures,
Jesus, Thy perfect likeness to wear.

Chorus: O to be like Thee! O to be like Thee!
Blessed Redeemer, pure as Thou art;
Come in Thy sweetness, come in Thy fullness;
Stamp Thine own image deep on my heart.

O to be like Thee! full of compassion,
Loving, forgiving, tender and kind,
Helping the helpless, cheering the fainting,
Seeking the wand'ring sinners to find.

O to be like Thee! lowly in spirit,
Holy and harmless, patient and brave;
Meekly enduring cruel reproaches,
Willing to suffer, others to save.

O to be like Thee! Lord, I am coming,
Now to receive th' anointing divine;
All that I am and have I am bringing;
Lord, from this moment all shall be Thine.

Another treasured, old hymn by Eliza E. Hewitt asks the questions, "Who will follow Jesus? Who will make reply, 'I am on the Lord's side, Master, here am I'?" Beginning this study, we humbly answer, "*I* want to follow Jesus. Master, here am I." And as we begin and throughout, we pray: "I cannot through my own strength do this. I look to You for strength, O Lord God my Father, through the name of Jesus my Savior."

3

ACKNOWLEDGE HIS DEITY

"I came forth from the Father and have come into the world;"
Matthew 16:28

WHAT JESUS CLAIMED:

Some say that Jesus never claimed to be deity, that this was a plot devised by his disciples after His death, but even His Jewish contemporaries recognized His assertions. Take for instance John 5:18: "For this reason therefore the Jews were seeking all the more to kill Him, because He not only was breaking the Sabbath, but also was calling God His own Father, making Himself equal with God." Consider also the words of Jesus in John 10:30, "I and the Father are one." Again the Jews' reaction shows they recognized that He was claiming to be God, picking up stones to stone Him, "because You, being a man, make Yourself out to be God" (John 10:33).

Perhaps His most powerful claim of all is recorded in John 8:56-59 when He asserted, "'Your father Abraham rejoiced to see My day, and he saw it and was glad.' [57] So the Jews said to Him, 'You are not yet fifty years old, and have You seen Abraham?' [58] Jesus said to them, 'Truly, truly, I say to you, before Abraham was born, I am.' [59] Therefore they picked up stones to throw at Him, but Jesus hid Himself and went out of the temple." The Jews' violent response to Jesus' claim to be "I AM" indicates that they recognized His assertion that He was the eternal God incarnate. Jesus was claiming the "I AM" name that God had used for Himself in Exodus 3:14

In Mark 14:61-64, at Jesus' trial, the high priest asked Him if He was the Christ. Jesus answered, "I am," and then He quoted from Daniel 7:13-14, "'And you shall see the Son of Man sitting at the right hand of power, and coming with the clouds of heaven.'" In response, He was condemned to death. If Jesus had not believed He was the Son of God, surely, He would have denied it at His trial.

When Peter made the confession, "You are the Christ, the Son of the living God," Jesus asserted that this truth came from the Father: "Blessed are you, Simon Barjona, because flesh and blood did not reveal this to you, but My Father who is in heaven" (Matthew 16:16-17). Martha, the friend of Jesus, made the same great confession after the death of her brother, Lazarus. "She said to Him, 'Yes, Lord; I have believed that You are the Christ, the Son of God, even He who comes into the world'" (John 11:27). Martha showed that she knew the Old Testament prophecies and recognized that Jesus fulfilled them, and Jesus did not deny it.

The apostle Thomas at first did not believe the report that Jesus had risen. But when he saw the hands and side of Jesus and believed, he declared, "My Lord and my God!" (John 20:28). Jesus did not correct him because He knew it to be true.

Jesus said, "He who has seen Me has seen the Father" (John 14:9). We cannot read the gospels and come to any other conclusion than that Jesus knew that He was the Son of God who had come to earth to do the will of the Father (John 5:19, 30). Thanks be to God that He devoted every moment of His life to that mission.

WHAT WE BELIEVE ABOUT HIS DEITY:

Belief in Jesus as deity, as the Son of God, is fundamental to our salvation. Jesus said in John 8:24, "Therefore I said to you that you will die in your sins; for unless you believe that I am He, you will die in your sins." In Mark 16:16, He told his apostles, "He who has believed and has been baptized shall be saved; but he who has disbelieved shall be condemned."

After Thomas had declared "My Lord and my God," Jesus said to him, "Because you have seen Me, you have believed. Blessed *are* those who have not seen and *yet* have believed." John then records: "Therefore many other signs Jesus also performed in the presence of the disciples, which are not written in this book; [31] but these have been written so that you may believe that Jesus is the Christ, the Son of God; and that believing you may have life in His name" (John 20:29-31). That is how we learn to believe.

Think of all that our belief in Jesus as the Son of God entails. We believe that Jesus is God, having every characteristic of God (Hebrews 1:3). We believe His every word is true and His every act is righteous and just. That His love is as the Father's love. Believing in Jesus means that we will submit our lives in devotion to Him as Lord and Master. Jesus showed the importance of obedience when He said, "Not everyone who says to Me, 'Lord, Lord,' will enter the kingdom of heaven, but he who does the will of My Father who is in heaven will enter" (Matthew 7:21). Believing in Jesus as God means doing His will.

The apostle Peter, who had closely walked and talked with Jesus, wrote, "And though you have not seen Him, you love Him, and though you do not see Him now, but believe in Him, you greatly rejoice with joy inexpressible and full of glory, [9] obtaining as the outcome of your faith the salvation of your souls" (1 Peter 1:8-9). That is how we believe in Jesus. We "rejoice with joy inexpressible and full of glory" because of our salvation which is the outcome of our faith.

Believing in Jesus as the Christ, the Son of God, is not a one-time act. We cannot say, "Now I believe, so I can check that off the list." We continually grow our faith by the Word of God. The Holy Spirit revealed to Christians, "But grow in the grace and knowledge of our Lord and Savior Jesus Christ" (2 Peter 3:18).

For Further Study: Is our belief strong? Is it strong enough to bend our will to God's? Is it strong enough to give up selfishness

6

and pride? Is it strong enough to give us joy? Let us reflect on our belief and how it impacts our lives. Read Hebrews 11, 1 John 5:5, and James 2:20.

HYMN

I Know That My Redeemer Lives F. Fillmore, Arranger, (1956) Public Domain

I know that my Redeemer Lives And ever prays for me; I know eternal life He gives, From sin and sorrow free.

Refrain: I know, I know that my Redeemer lives, I know, I know eternal life he gives; I know, I know that my Redeemer lives.

He wills that I should holy be, In word, and tho't, in deed; Then I His holy face may see, When from this earth-life freed. [Refrain]

I know that unto sinful men His saving grace is nigh; I know that He will come again To take me home on high. [Refrain]

I know that over yonder stands A place prepared for me; A home, a house not made with hands, Most wonderful to see. [Refrain]

ARMED FOR BATTLE

"The LORD reigns, He is clothed with majesty;
The LORD has clothed and girded Himself with strength;"
Psalm 93:1

HOW JESUS WAS ARMED:

The first promise from God to send a victor over Satan came in Genesis 3:15 after the first sin. God promised that One born of woman, would battle with Satan, crush his head, and defeat him.

Throughout the Old Testament God reaffirmed His promise. In Zephaniah 3:16-17, it was prophesied of Him, "In that day it will be said to Jerusalem: 'Do not be afraid, O Zion; Do not let your hands fall limp. [17]The Lord your God is in your midst, A victorious warrior. He will exult over you with joy, He will be quiet in His love, He will rejoice over you with shouts of joy.'"

The promise of a coming warrior was to give the people courage. Israel's history was one of warfare, so, when the Lord promised a powerful warrior to do battle for them, it was a promise with which they could relate. No weak warrior was coming! He would prevail over their enemies! See the warrior described in Isaiah 42:13: "The LORD will go forth like a warrior, He will arouse His zeal like a man of war. He will utter a shout, yes, He will raise a war cry. He will prevail against His enemies."

The Holy Spirit through Isaiah showed that the warrior would be armed for battle. In Isaiah 59:17, he says, "He put on righteousness like a breastplate, And a helmet of salvation on His head; And He put on garments of vengeance for clothing And

8

wrapped Himself with zeal as a mantle." In 11: 5, Isaiah says, "Also righteousness will be the belt about His loins, And faithfulness the belt about His waist." See what the Divine Warrior would be wearing. He is suited for spiritual battle with righteousness, salvation, vengeance, zeal, and faithfulness. Does He not sound like someone that you would want to battle for you?

When the great Warrior Jesus came to earth, many rejected Him because they were looking for a literal warrior king who would restore Israel as a powerful earthly nation. Yet Jesus came to earth to do spiritual battle with Satan as prophesied in Genesis 3:15. From the time of His birth, when the angel proclaimed, "For today in the city of David there has been born for you a Savior, who is Christ the Lord" (Luke 2:11), it was both declared and demonstrated that this was the Messiah, the Warrior that had come to save man from the powers of Satan.

Jesus the King came prepared for battle, ready to fight for us, to slay the enemy. And yes, the Warrior was victorious, winning the battle over Satan, living a perfect sinless life (Hebrews 4:15, 1 Peter 2:22, 2 Corinthians 5:21), then offering Himself as a sacrifice for our sins. He fought a battle for us that we could not win ourselves. Let us thank God for His victory.

Remember that the enemy whom Jesus fought against is our enemy as well. 1 Peter 5:8 says, "Be of sober spirit, be on the alert. Your adversary, the devil, prowls around like a roaring lion, seeking someone to devour."

HOW WE ARE TO BE ARMED:

In the same way that the Father armed His Son for battle with Satan, He also equips the Christian for battle with him. In Ephesians 6, the apostle Paul paints a picture of our armor. He says in verses 10-11, "Finally, be strong in the Lord and in the strength of His might. [11] Put on the full armor of God, so that you will be able to stand firm against the schemes of the devil." This armor, the same as the Warrior wore, enables us to be "strong in the Lord and in the strength of His might." We too can be powerful warriors, just as Jesus was, not in our strength but in the Lord's.

Even though God provides this powerful armor, notice that *we* must put it on. In verses 14-17, Paul states, "Stand firm therefore, having [1] *girded* [emphasis ours] your loins with truth, and having [2] *put on* the breastplate of righteousness, [15] and having [3] *shod* your feet with the preparation of the gospel of peace; [16] in addition to all, [4] *taking up* the shield of faith with which you will be able to extinguish all the flaming arrows of the evil one. [17] And [5] *take* the helmet of salvation, and the [6] sword of the Spirit, which is the word of God." God provides the armor, but it cannot protect us unless we put it on.

Truth, righteousness, the gospel, faith, salvation, and the word of God are our protection against Satan. When we wear these, we are not weak warriors. We are instead strong in the mighty power of God. When the youth David fought Goliath he said, "And I will give the dead bodies of the Philistines this day to the birds of the sky and the wild beasts of the earth, that all the earth may know that there is a God in Israel, [47] and that all this assembly may know that the LORD does not deliver by sword or by spear; for the battle is the LORD'S and He will give you into our hands" (1 Samuel 17:46b-47). Let us remember when we wear His armor, "the battle is the Lord's."

For Further Study: Read Hebrews 4:12, 1 Thessalonians 5:8, 1 Peter 5:8-9, 1 John 5:4-5, Isaiah 52:7, 1 Peter 1:13, 2 Corinthians 10:4

Hymn

Soldiers of Christ Arise C. Wesley (1749) Public Domain

Soldiers of Christ, arise,
And put your armor on,
Strong in the strength which God supplies (repeat)
Through His beloved Son.

Strong in the Lord of hosts,
And in His mighty pow'r,
Who in the strength of Jesus trusts (repeat)
Is more than conqueror.

Stand then in His great might,
With all His strength endued,
And take, to arm you for the fight, (repeat)
The panoply of God;

That, having all things done,
And all your conflicts passed,
Ye may o'ercome through Christ alone, (repeat)
And stand entire at last.

Leave no unguarded place,
No weakness of the soul,
Take every virtue, every grace, (repeat)
And fortify the whole

BE BOLD

"That we confidently say, 'The Lord is my helper, I will not be afraid. What will man do to me?'" Hebrews 13:6

HOW JESUS WAS BOLD:

Boldness is defined as "action in spite of danger." How many times do we read that Jesus, in spite of danger, confronted those in power with the truth? His words often angered the religious leaders of His day to the point that they wanted to put him to death, yet He frequently stood up to them publicly and boldly pointed out their hypocrisy and self-righteousness.

Consider what boldness it took for Jesus to say to the religious leaders in Matthew 21:31, "Truly I say to you that the tax collectors and prostitutes will get into the kingdom of God before you." In Matthew 23:13-36 we find some of the most severe words spoken by Jesus. He begins by saying in verse 13, "But woe to you, scribes and Pharisees, hypocrites, because you shut off the kingdom of heaven from people; for you do not enter in yourselves, nor do you allow those who are entering to go in." Seven more woes followed, woe upon woe.

Why was Jesus so stern with them? He knew their hearts and what they needed to hear, and that is what He delivered. When the people needed a gentle message, they received it. Likewise, when the Jewish leaders needed a stern rebuke, they received it. They had rejected Him as the promised Messiah and led the people away from God. Did Jesus enjoy rebuking the leaders? The very next verse (37) tells us, "Jerusalem, Jerusalem, who kills the prophets and stones those who are sent to her! How often I wanted to gather your children together, the way a hen gathers her chicks under her wings, and you were unwilling."

But Jesus had a heart to please God regardless and was willing to face the dangers. Turning people's hearts to God was what was important to Him. "For the Son of Man came to seek and to save the lost" (Luke 19:10), and He would let no dangers thwart that cause.

Faithful men and women of scriptures also exhibited boldness like Jesus. They confronted kings if necessary and chose to suffer persecution rather than keep silent. Consider Elijah. Desiring to kill him, King Ahab had been searching for Elijah far and wide. God told Elijah to go and show himself to the King. Even though it could have been fatal, Elijah obeyed the Lord without hesitation. When he faced Ahab, Elijah called him a "troubler of Israel" and charged: "You have forsaken the commandments of the Lord and you have followed the Baals" (I Kings 18:17-18). What a profound example of boldness!

What of Esther who risked her life to approach her husband, King Xerxes, to foil Haman's plans to annihilate the Jews (Esther 4). Esther knew of the dangers of approaching the king without his request. But her uncle Mordecai beseeched her with that great statement, "And who knows whether you have not attained royalty for such a time as this?" When Esther decided to intercede, she requested a three-day fast of all the people, then boldly said, "And thus I will go in to the king, which is not according to the law; and if I perish, I perish" (Esther 4:16). We thank God for such an impressive example of boldness.

HOW WE MUST BE BOLD:

In the same way, we must let nothing prevent our defense of the gospel. Peter encourages us to be bold in 1 Peter 3:13-15: "Who is there to harm you if you prove zealous for what is good? [14] But even if you should suffer for the sake of righteousness, you are blessed. And do not fear their intimidation, and do not be troubled, [15] but sanctify Christ as Lord in your hearts, always being ready to

13

make a defense to everyone who asks you to give an account for the hope that is in you, yet with gentleness and reverence."

In Acts 3-4, Peter and John were arrested and forced to stand trial before the same court that weeks before had condemned Jesus. When the court released them, they warned Peter and John with grave threats not to preach anymore in the name of Jesus. Returning to the church, Peter and John related what had happened, and they all prayed together. They could have asked God to deliver them from the rulers or to keep them safe. Yet they did not, not at all. Rather they prayed, "Now, Lord, look on their threats, and grant to Your servants that with all boldness they may speak Your word." (Acts 4:29 NKJV). What a moving prayer of faith. Let us pray that we will be bold.

In Hebrews 13:6 the writer says, "So that we confidently say, 'The Lord is my helper, I will not be afraid. What will man do to me?'" This reveals the source of our boldness. Just prior to this in verse five, the scripture says, "for He Himself has said, 'I will never desert you, nor will I ever forsake you.'" God's promise is real, and all that is left is for us to believe it and act boldly upon it.

Proverbs 28:1 says, "The wicked flee when no one pursues, but the righteous are bold as a lion." How bold are lions? They do not cringe before anything. We can be that bold because we know that God is for us. The apostle Paul, while in prison, wrote to the church of Ephesus asking them to pray, not for his release, but that "I may speak boldly, as I ought to speak" (Ephesians 6:19-20).

Certainly, boldness is not always easy. Think of Deborah in Judges 4 confronting Sisera's imposing army. What gave her boldness? She says to Israel's army, "Arise! For this is the day in which the LORD has given Sisera into your hands; behold, the LORD has gone out before you" (verse 14). Her boldness comes from her great faith in God. And that is where our boldness comes.

For Further Study Are we ever too timid to speak up for Jesus? Pray for boldness. Remember God is the source, not us. Make a list of others in scripture or that you have known who boldly stood for God. Really consider the words of this well-loved old hymn.

HYMN

Stand up, Stand up for Jesus G. Duffield (1858) Public Domain

Stand up, stand up for Jesus ye soldiers of the cross;
lift high his royal banner, it must not suffer loss.
From vict'ry unto vict'ry his army shall he lead
till ev'ry foe is vanquished and Christ is Lord indeed.

Stand up, stand up for Jesus, the trumpet call obey;
forth to the mighty conflict in this his glorious day.
Ye that are men now serve him against unnumbered foes;
let courage rise with danger and strength to strength oppose.

Stand up, stand up for Jesus, stand in his strength alone;
the arm of flesh will fail you, ye dare not trust your own.
Put on the gospel armor, each piece put on with prayer;
where duty calls or danger, be never wanting there.

Stand up, stand up for Jesus, the strife will not be long;
this day the noise of battle, the next, the victor's song.
To him that overcometh a crown of life shall be;
And with the King of glory shall reign eternally.

GIVE COMFORT

"The LORD is near to the brokenhearted And saves those who
are crushed in spirit." Psalm 34:18

HOW JESUS GIVES COMFORT:

Struggles are a real part of Christians' lives. If we think the
Christian life will be without struggle, we are wrong. Temptation,
sin, persecution, sickness and death of loved ones are just a few of
the heartaches that we will face. But God will give us comfort in all
our struggles if we will let Him.

Our lesson, *Mourn like Jesus* (page #109), emphasizes how we
should mourn over our sins, but God does not want us to continue
to mourn forever. Consider how distraught David was in Psalm 51
over his sin, praying, "For I know my transgressions, And my sin is
always before me" (verse 3). Then in verse 12 he prays, "Restore to
me the joy of Your salvation And sustain me with a willing spirit."
God's forgiveness is a soothing salve to our emotional wounds,
giving comfort.

Early Christians lived in perilous times. Paul writes of his
sufferings and the comfort he receives from God in 2 Corinthians
1:3-7: "Blessed be the God and Father of our Lord Jesus Christ, the
Father of mercies and God of all comfort, [4] who comforts us in all
our affliction so that we will be able to comfort those who are in
any affliction with the comfort with which we ourselves are
comforted by God. [5] For just as the sufferings of Christ are ours in
abundance, so also our comfort is abundant through Christ. [6] But if
we are afflicted, it is for your comfort and salvation; or if we are
comforted, it is for your comfort, which is effective in the patient
enduring of the same sufferings which we also suffer; [7] and our
hope for you is firmly grounded, knowing that as you are sharers of
our sufferings, so also you are sharers of our comfort."

The word translated as comfort here, *paraklesis,* has the root meaning of coming alongside someone to give assistance. It is the same concept Jesus used when He described sending the Comforter, the Holy Spirit. It is more than just momentary relief, but it is sustained strengthening and encouragement. Paul strongly believed that even though the Corinthians would suffer, they would also be comforted. He says his hope for the Corinthians in this is "firmly grounded." Who gives this comfort? "The Father of mercies and God of all comfort." It is "abundant through Christ." We are going to suffer in this life. But God will give us *abundant* comfort if we turn to Him.

The psalmist in Psalm 119:50 says, "This is my comfort in my affliction, That Your word has revived me." Do we let God's word revive us when we are troubled? Most of us look to other people, who can indeed be encouraging. But how can anything be more comforting than verses such as, "Now may the God of hope fill you with all joy and peace in believing, so that you will abound in hope by the power of the Holy Spirit" (Romans 15:13)?

Remember the hymn *Does Jesus Care?* (Frank E. Graeff). It asks, "Does Jesus care" in various painful situations. For instance, "Does Jesus care when I've tried and failed to resist some temptation strong." And from 1 Peter 5:7 we know the answer: "Casting all your anxiety on Him, because He cares for you." "Oh yes, He cares. I know He cares." What comfort that gives. The great God of the universe cares for us and comforts us.

HOW WE GIVE COMFORT:

In 1 Corinthians 5, Paul instructed the church to discipline an erring brother. Then in 2 Corinthians 2, we read that the brother had repented. Paul then tells the church to comfort the brother, and to reaffirm their love to him, "so that on the contrary you should rather forgive and comfort him, otherwise such a one might be overwhelmed by excessive sorrow" (2 Corinthians 2:7).

Mourning turns to rejoicing. Jesus closed the parable of the Lost Sheep with this: "'Rejoice with me, for I have found my sheep which was lost!' I tell you that in the same way, there will be more joy in heaven over one sinner who repents than over ninety-nine righteous persons who need no repentance" (Luke 15:6b-7). We love to see a long line of brothers and sisters waiting their turn to encourage, comfort and reaffirm their love to one who has confessed sins. It is one way that we show our comfort and love.

Today we hear Christians say, "I know God has forgiven me, but I cannot forgive myself." This sounds a lot like being "overwhelmed by excessive sorrow" that Paul warned about. We must help Christians overcome this way of thinking and truly thank God for His forgiveness. Let us help them see that to fully please God, we must accept the comfort of forgiveness that He imparts.

Sinning against God is a horrible, painful thing. Imagine how Peter felt when Jesus gazed at him after he had denied Him. The Scriptures say he went out and wept bitterly (Luke 22:62). As painful as that was for Peter, he did not let it keep him from becoming a worthy servant in the kingdom. Think of the apostle Paul, who had persecuted Christians. When he accepted Christ, he did not let his past keep him from working diligently for Jesus.

Another way that we comfort brethren is over the loss of a loved one. In 1 Thessalonians 4:13, Paul instructs us, "But we do not want you to be uninformed, brethren, about those who are asleep, so that you will not grieve as do the rest who have no hope." The death of a loved one can be a source of distress, but the apostle comforts with the assurance that "we shall always be with the Lord" (verse 17). Then he concludes with: "Therefore comfort one another with these words" (verse 18). What healing comfort that is!

For Further Study: Think of others that are hurting to whom you could give comfort. Time and effort are all it costs.

HYMN

Redeemed Fanny Crosby (1882) Public Domain

Redeemed, how I love to proclaim it!
Redeemed by the blood of the Lamb;
Redeemed through His infinite mercy,
His child, and forever, I am.

Refrain: Redeemed, redeemed,
Redeemed by the blood of the Lamb;
Redeemed, redeemed!
His child, and forever, I am

I think of my blessed Redeemer,
I think of Him all the day long;
I sing, for I cannot be silent;
His love is the theme of my song. [Refrain]

I know I shall see in His beauty
The King in whose law I delight,
Who lovingly guardeth my footsteps,
And giveth me songs in the night. [Refrain]

BE COMMITTED

"You shall love the Lord your God with all your heart, and with all your soul, and with all your mind." Mt. 22:37

HOW JESUS WAS COMMITTED:

Commitment is defined as "the state or quality of being dedicated to a cause, person, etc." We sometimes speak of "total commitment" and need look no further than Jesus to find it.

On the cross, after having fulfilled His purpose, Jesus cried out with a loud voice, "'Father, into Your hands I commit My spirit.' Having said this, He breathed His last" (Luke 23:46). The Greek word translated "commit" means to place with someone or to entrust. In total commitment, Jesus placed His spirit into the care of the tender, loving hands of his Father. This is the fulfillment of the words in Psalm 31:5: "Into Your hand I commit my spirit; You have ransomed me, O LORD, God of truth."S

If we look back at the life of Jesus to see how He was able to fulfill His purpose with such unwavering commitment, we see that He lived in complete trust and obedience to His Father. Jesus said in John 4:34, "My food is to do the will of Him who sent Me and to accomplish His work." Food is our sustenance. It is what fortifies and keeps us going. Notice other times that He says He has come to do the will of the Father (John 5:30; 6:38; 8:26; 10:1; 12:49-50; 14:30-31; 15:10). He was totally committed to His Father's will, even "to the point of death, even death on a cross" (Philippians 2:8b).

Total commitment prompted Jesus at all times, in all things, and in all ways to seek God's will. Even at twelve years old, He asked His mother when they found Him in the temple, "Why did you seek Me? Did you not know that I must be about My Father's business?" (Luke 2:49 NKJV).

Jesus also never wavered from His commitment to us. "Christ also loved you and gave Himself up for us, an offering and a sacrifice to God as a fragrant aroma" (Ephesians 5:2). As we read the gospels, Matthew through John, we never see a moment of half-heartedness or selfishness from Jesus. We see in His every step an absolute determination to sacrifice Himself for us. The night before his arrest, Jesus pleads to the Father for release from his burden if it is God's will. Jesus prays "Father, if You are willing, remove this cup from Me; yet not My will, but Yours be done" (Luke 22:42). But God didn't take the weight from him, and the next day Jesus died, praying those words, "Father, into Your hands I commit My spirit." Jesus did not relish the horrible ordeal to come, but was willing for the Father and for us.

In Hebrews 12:2 the Spirit revealed that Jesus "endured the cross, despising the shame." That doesn't mean he hated the shame but that it meant nothing to Him. His sacrificial death on the cross completed the mission of God to bring men back to Him. Then in the next verse: "For consider Him who has endured such hostility by sinners against Himself, so that you will not grow weary and lose heart." We should look to Jesus if we want to see a commitment that inspires us to keep our own commitment strong. What kind of commitment would you say it would take for Jesus to endure all he did? There are hardly words to describe it. Thank God for Jesus' total commitment.

OUR COMMITMENT:

Are we determined to commit to God like Jesus did, in full obedience and in complete devotion to fulfilling His purpose for us? We must understand that this commitment we make to God is not just one time when we accept Christ as our Savior and are baptized into Him, but a daily, hourly, sometimes moment-by-moment dedication. If we are not careful and do not constantly focus, in weak moments temptations can gain the upper hand, or the cares of the world can choke out our interest in the Lord as we give little thought to Him. So how do we totally commit ourselves to God?

Perhaps the scripture that first comes to mind when we think of total commitment to God is when Jesus said, "You shall love the Lord your God with all your heart, and with all your soul, and with all your mind. [38] This is the great and foremost commandment" (Matthew 22:37). Love the Lord with everything that we are. First and foremost, our commitment hinges on our love for God

To love God with our whole being, we must exercise that love. We may not wake up every morning with our heart focused on the Lord, eager to do His will but rather may be so busy starting our day that He does not even cross our minds. But we can remedy that. Determine to pray a prayer of thanksgiving every morning before we rise. When the alarm rings, pray, "Thank you, Lord, for this day. Today I seek to do Your will." Lay your Bible where you will see it so you won't forget. Leave a note on your refrigerator. When you start to pick up your phone, first turn your thoughts to God's love and rejoice in His righteousness and mercy.

No one is reading these words and saying, "Well, this is easy—no problem." No, to put God's will before our own is a life-long struggle. Some days are harder than others: selfish days, proudful days, lustful days. Those are hard, but God is here, wanting us, pursuing us, seeking us, helping us, and forgiving us. Some days were hard even for Jesus, were they not?

For Further Study: Do a self-examination. What stands between us and total commitment to God? What can we do today to be more committed than yesterday? What can we do tomorrow, if there be a tomorrow? How can we grow in our commitment?

HYMN

When I Survey the Wondrous Cross I. Watts (1707), Public Domain

When I survey the wondrous cross
On which the Prince of glory died,
My richest gain I count but loss,
And pour contempt on all my pride.

Forbid it, Lord, that I should boast,
Save in the death of Christ my Lord!
All the vain things that charm me most,
I sacrifice them to His blood.

See from His head, His hands, His feet,
Sorrow and love flow mingled down!
Did e'er such love and sorrow meet,
Or thorns compose so rich a crown?

Were the whole realm of nature mine,
That were a present far too small;
Love so amazing, so divine,
Demands my soul, my life, my all.

SHOW COMPASSION

"Gracious is the LORD, and righteous; Yes, our God
is compassionate." Psalm 116:5

HOW JESUS SHOWS COMPASSION:

In James 5:11, the Spirit makes a declaration about God's character: "The Lord is full of compassion and is merciful." According to Vine's, compassion is "to be moved as to one's inwards." We would say "to be cut to the heart". What a tremendous thought: that this is how the Lord feels about us. Psalm 103:8 says, "The LORD is compassionate and gracious, Slow to anger and abounding in lovingkindness." Thank God for His compassion.

The Lord describes Himself as compassionate in Exodus 34:6: "Then the LORD passed by in front of him and proclaimed, 'The LORD, the LORD God, compassionate and gracious, slow to anger, and abounding in lovingkindness and truth.'" This description is repeated by prophets throughout the Old Testament (Deuteronomy 4:31; 2 Chronicles 30:9; Nehemiah 9:17,31; Psalm 78:38; Psalm 103:8; Psalm 111:4; Psalm 112:4; Psalm 116:5; Joel 2:13). Remember, this was Jonah's explanation of why he did not want to go to Nineveh to preach, "for I knew that You are a gracious and compassionate God, slow to anger and abundant in lovingkindness, and one who relents concerning calamity" (Jonah 4:2). Jonah implies that he suspected God would not carry out their destruction but would forgive them when they repented.

It was this deep compassion that brought Jesus to earth to die for us. Compassion is more than sympathy or empathy but is action based on that emotion. Jesus did not merely look down on us in sympathy from his heavenly throne. Compassion moved Him to leave heaven and come to earth so that we could one day be in heaven with Him.

Christ was frequently moved with compassion:

Luke 7:13: When the Lord saw her, He felt compassion for her, and said to her, "Do not weep."

Matthew 14:14: When He went ashore, He saw a large crowd, and felt compassion for them and healed their sick.

Matthew 15:32: And Jesus called His disciples to Him, and said, "I feel compassion for the people, because they have remained with me now three days and have nothing to eat; and I do not want to send them away hungry, for they might faint on the way."

Matthew 9:36: Seeing the people, He felt compassion for them, because they were distressed and dispirited like sheep without a shepherd.

Matthew 20:34: Moved with compassion, Jesus touched their eyes; and immediately they regained their sight and followed Him.

Mark 1:41: Moved with compassion, Jesus reached out His hand and touched him, and said to him, "I am willing; be cleansed."

Luke 15:20: So he got up and came to his father. But while he was still a long way off, his father saw him and felt compassion for him, and ran and embraced him and kissed him.

We can hear the compassion in the voice of Jesus when He said on the cross: "Father, forgive them; for they do not know what they are doing" (Luke 23:34). Do we not know that He feels that same compassion as He looks down on us today?

HOW WE SHOW COMPASSION:

In Philippians 2:1-2, the Spirit exhorts us to emulate Christ's compassion. Paul says, "Therefore if there is any encouragement in

Christ, if there is any consolation of love, if there is any fellowship of the Spirit, if any affection and compassion, [2] make my joy complete by being of the same mind, maintaining the same love, united in spirit, intent on one purpose." "If there is any!" Of course, there is abundant encouragement, comfort, affection, and so forth in Christ. Since these are obvious in Christ, then the results—compassion, unity, love, and cooperation—should be just as obvious in us. It is another exhortation to be like Jesus.

How can we not be moved when we read the parable of the Good Samaritan of Luke 10? Jesus was asked by a temple official, a lawyer, "Who is my neighbor?" and He replied with a parable. He told of a man going from Jerusalem to Jericho who fell among robbers. They stripped him and beat him and departed, leaving him half dead. Then he told of two religious people, a priest and a Levite, who saw him but passed by on the other side. One of Jesus' criticisms of the Jewish leaders was their hypocrisy. Here was another example of it.

Then He continued, "But a Samaritan, who was on a journey, came upon him; and when he saw him, he felt compassion, [34] and came to him and bandaged up his wounds, pouring oil and wine on them; and he put him on his own beast, and brought him to an inn and took care of him. [35] On the next day he took out two denarii and gave them to the innkeeper and said, "Take care of him; and whatever more you spend, when I return I will pay you.""" The parable's lesson is that those who *show* compassion, not just claim to be religious, are those who please God.

Notice how Jesus ended the parable asking, "Which of these three do you think proved to be a neighbor to the man who fell into the robbers' hands?" It is obvious, is it not? It was the hated Samaritan who showed mercy. Then Jesus told them to go and do the same. That is our lesson, also, to do the same. Like the good Samaritan, compassionate people do not merely sympathize and empathize, but they also help alleviate the sufferings of others. Compassion is caring, and also doing.

Colossians 3:12-13 says to us: "So, as those who have been chosen of God, holy and beloved, put on a heart of compassion, kindness, humility, gentleness and patience; [13]bearing with one another, and forgiving each other, whoever has a complaint against anyone; just as the Lord forgave you, so also should you." He says, "Put on a heart of compassion." A heart of compassion will care and act. As we seek to be more like Jesus, let us be "moved with compassion" to help others.

Can we have more compassion for those in sin? Can we realize that "there but for the grace of God go I"? Can we look around to see who might need our care? And remember, sometimes "just a small kindly deed that may cheer another is the work God has planned for you" ("Room in God's Kingdom," J.R. Baxter, Jr.) In the words of Jesus our Master in Matthew 10:42: "And whoever in the name of a disciple gives to one of these little ones even a cup of cold water to drink, truly I say to you, he shall not lose his reward."

For Further Study: In Matthew 9:13, Jesus told the Pharisees, "'But go and learn what this means: "I desire compassion, and not sacrifice," for I did not come to call the righteous, but sinners.'" Research this quotation.

BE COURAGEOUS

"For the battle is the Lord's and He will give you into our hands."
I Samuel 17:47

HOW JESUS WAS COURAGEOUS:

Perhaps John Wayne had the best description of courage when he said, as it is claimed, "Courage is being scared to death but saddling up anyway." Webster defines courage as "mental or moral strength to venture, persevere, and withstand danger." Many, many times Jesus courageously withstood danger.

Consider Jesus' courage during His arrest, trial, and crucifixion. Knowing what was to transpire, He could have prevented it. On the way to Jerusalem, He rehearsed to his apostles: "Behold, we are going up to Jerusalem, and the Son of Man will be delivered to the chief priests and the scribes; and they will condemn Him to death and will hand Him over to the Gentiles. [34] They will mock Him and spit on Him, and scourge Him and kill Him, and three days later He will rise again" (Mark 10:33-34). When they came to arrest him, Jesus said, "Or do you think that I cannot appeal to My Father, and He will at once put at My disposal more than twelve legions of angels?" (Matthew 26:53).

Jesus did not relish humiliation or pain any more than we do. In the garden with Peter, James, and John, when He went to pray, the Scriptures say He "began to be grieved and distressed. Then He said to them, 'My soul is deeply grieved, to the point of death; remain here and keep watch with Me.'" (Matthew 26:37b-38).

Jesus could have struck the soldiers down when they came for Him, but Jesus endured what was before Him. He willingly submitted to the degradation done to Him, "so that He might bring us to God" (1 Peter 3:18). Consider that expression: "bring us to God." Jesus' courage came from his desire to fulfill God's purpose to save man. For this we must praise and thank Him.

HOW WE CAN BE COURAGEOUS:

Thanks be to God, we do not have to fear government forces who would oppose our service to God, but that does not mean that it does not take courage to serve Him. Perhaps we have opposition from family members, or we experience ridicule from co-workers for our beliefs. Even children have been punished by coaches or teachers when they put serving God before secular activities.

As the world departs more and more from biblical principles, the more that Christians require courage to oppose sin. When sin is condoned and even promoted, it is harder to resist. Alcohol and drugs, pornography and other sexual sins are rampant in our society. Aggression and violence are everyday occurrences. God is not revered. Sin often surrounds us at our workplace or school.

So how do we avoid sin when we are surrounded by it? Jesus was not cowering in the garden, hiding in fear, when the soldiers came for Him. Rather, He had gone to a quiet place to commune with the source of His courage, put on His armor, and prepare for His battle (Isaiah 42:13). As Jesus did, so we should also do. "Finally, be strong in the Lord and in the strength of His might. 11Put on the full armor of God, so that you will be able to stand firm against the schemes of the devil. 12 For our struggle is not against flesh and blood, but against the rulers, against the powers, against the world forces of this darkness, against the spiritual forces of wickedness in the heavenly places" (Ephesians 6:10-12).

If we would only realize the source of our courage! Let us look at one of the most famous stories of all time in 1 Samuel 17 – David and Goliath. Every day, Goliath, a massive man, had taunted the army of Israel to accept his fight-to-the-death, winner-takes-all challenge. Every morning when he stepped forward, the men of God shrank back in fear until a young shepherd, David, came, heard the taunts, and took up the challenge, saying to Goliath, "This day the LORD will deliver you up into my hands, and I will strike you down and remove your head from you. And I will give the dead bodies of the army of the Philistines this day to the birds of the sky and the wild beasts of the earth, that all the earth may know that there is a God in Israel, [47]and that all this assembly may know that the Lord does not deliver by sword or by spear; for the battle is the Lord's and He will give you into our hands" (1 Samuel 17:46-47).

So was this a self-confident young man? No, his confidence lay in God. David saw God as more powerful than the feared Philistine, so he went out to fight, believing that God would give him victory. That faith gave David courage, and that kind of faith can give us courage. Never let any "Goliath" loom larger than God.

We are all different. Fear is more challenging for some than for others, but we all face situations where we feel timid or afraid. Some fear criticism. Others are afraid of confrontation, others of being made to look foolish, and others of rejection. Let us gird up for battle with the following thought: "Be on the alert, stand firm in the faith, act like men, be strong" (1 Corinthians 16:13).

The apostle Paul encouraged Timothy this way: "For God has not given us a spirit of timidity, but of power and love and discipline. [8]Therefore do not be ashamed of the testimony of our Lord or of me His prisoner but join with me in suffering for the gospel according to the power of God" (2 Timothy 1:7-8).

For Further Study: Do a self-reflection. Where do you need more courage? Pray for courage to overcome. Read these verses that tell us to be strong and courageous: Deuteronomy 31:6-7, 23; Joshua 1:6-7,9, 18; Joshua 10:25; 2 Samuel 10:12; 1 Chronicles 19:13; 1 Chronicles 22:13; 1 Chronicles 28:20; and 2 Chronicles 32:7.

HYMN

To Christ Be True E. Hoffman (1928) Public Domain

To Christ be loyal and be true; His banner be unfurled,
And borne aloft till is secured The conquest of the world.

To Christ be loyal and be true; He needs brave volunteers
To stand against the pow'rs of sin, Moved not by frowns or fears.

To Christ be loyal and be true; In noble service prove
Your faith and your fidelity, The fervor of your love.

To Christ be loyal and be true, And He will be your friend,
Defending and protecting you To life's triumphant end.

Chorus: To Christ, the Lord, be true, For He will go with you, And help you all your conflicts thru; To Christ, the Lord, be true.

CRUCIFIED AND RESURRECTED

"Therefore we have been buried with Him through baptism into death, so that as Christ was raised from the dead through the glory of the Father, so we too might walk in newness of life."
Romans 6:4

AS JESUS WAS:

Salvation requires not only the *physical* crucifixion and resurrection of Jesus but also the *spiritual* crucifixion and resurrection of man.

Jesus' crucifixion and resurrection was the pivotal act of history, with eternal impact on all humanity. "For while we were still helpless, at the right time Christ died for the ungodly" (Romans 5:6). It was the most selfless act of love ever conceived. "But God demonstrates His own love toward us, in that while we were yet sinners, Christ died for us" (Romans 5:8). We should not let a day go by that we do not praise God and thank Jesus for His love.

Paul proclaimed it of "first importance." "Now I make known to you, brethren, the gospel which I preached to you, which also you received, in which also you stand, ²by which also you are saved, if you hold fast the word which I preached to you, unless you believed in vain. ³For I delivered to you as of first importance what I also received, that Christ died for our sins according to the Scriptures" (1 Corinthians 15:1-3). It is this on which we stand.

The resurrection of Jesus Christ validates who Jesus claimed to be, namely, the Son of God and Messiah. In Matthew 16, despite Jesus having just cured a demon-possessed, blind, and deaf man, the Pharisees asked for a "sign from heaven," miraculous proof that He was indeed the Messiah. Jesus answered, "An evil and adulterous generation seeks after a sign; and a sign will not be given it, except the sign of Jonah" (Matthew 16:4). Jesus used the phrase "sign of Jonah" as a metaphor for His future time in the grave, then His resurrection. *That* was their sign. The resurrection of Jesus Christ, attested to by hundreds of eyewitnesses (1 Corinthians 15:4-8), provides irrefutable proof that He is the Savior of the world.

We read the full accounts of the crucifixion and resurrection of Jesus in Matthew 26-28, Mark 15-16, Luke 22-24, and John 17-20. To do so is both faith-building and spirit-building. Reading it conveys to us the enormity of the Lord's love for us that He would endure such horror at the hands of man. Jesus did not die a peaceful death at old age. He was crucified, a form of execution intended not just to bring on death, but to inflict agonizing pain. Think of the word "excruciating" which is derived from crucifixion. Let us consider prayerfully what He endured for us.

We were all in sin, lost, separated from God. Jesus brought us back to Him. "Therefore, having been justified by faith, we have peace with God through our Lord Jesus Christ, [2] through whom also we have obtained our introduction by faith into this grace in which we stand; and we exult in hope of the glory of God" (Romans 5:1-2). Exult means to feel or show triumphant elation or jubilation. This hope in the glory of God is why the Ethiopian eunuch went on his way rejoicing after he was baptized into Christ (Acts 8:39). It is also why we are to "rejoice in the Lord always" (Philippians 4:4). We thank God with jubilation for this tremendous hope.

HOW WE ARE CRUCIFIED AND RESURRECTED:

Let us carefully study Romans 6:2b-6. It describes how we spiritually die, are buried, and resurrected with Christ through baptism.

"How shall we who died to sin still live in it? ³ Or do you not know that all of us who have been baptized into Christ Jesus have been baptized into His death? ⁴ Therefore we have been buried with Him through baptism into death, so that as Christ was raised from the dead through the glory of the Father, so we too might walk in newness of life. ⁵ For if we have become united with Him in the likeness of His death, certainly we shall also be in the likeness of His resurrection, ⁶ knowing this, that our old self was crucified with Him, in order that our body of sin might be done away with, so that we would no longer be slaves to sin."

This passage teaches us how we get into Christ, yet its primary purpose is to teach Christians to live free from sin. When we were immersed, we went through a spiritual crucifixion and resurrection. Our old self was crucified. We then died to sin and were raised to walk a new life. We cannot claim to be new creatures and live the old life of sin.

In Galatians 2:20 Paul proclaimed, "I have been crucified with Christ; and it is no longer I who live, but Christ lives in me; and the life which I now live in the flesh I live by faith in the Son of God, who loved me and gave Himself up for me." What a compelling statement this is about our new way of life. Think of it: we are letting Christ rule our lives. 2 Corinthians 5:17 says, "Therefore if anyone is in Christ, he is a new creature; the old things passed away; behold, new things have come."

What a glorious thought—the old, sinful self dies and is buried in baptism, and a new man is resurrected. Imagine if we still had all our old sins on our backs. We are free from them through God's grace.

For Further Study: Find hymns and other scriptures about the new life in Christ.

HYMN

A New Creature T. Chisholm (1933) Public Domain

Buried with Christ, my blessed Redeemer,
Dead to the old life of folly and sin;
Satan may call, the world may entreat me,
There is no voice that answers within.

Refrain: Dead to the world, to voices that call me,
Living anew, obedient but free;
Dead to the joys that once did enthrall me,
Yet 'tis not I, Christ liveth in me.

Think it not strange that things I once cherished
Cannot allure me or charm as before;
For in the flesh with Christ I have suffered,
Old things are passed, I love them no more. Refrain

Dead unto sin, alive through the Spirit,
Risen with Him from the gloom of the grave,
All things are new, and I am rejoicing
In His great love, His power to save. Refrain

Sin hath no more its cruel dominion,
Walking "in newness of life," I am free;
Glorious life of Christ, my Redeemer,
Which He so richly shareth with me. Refrain

DIE

"Even though I walk through the valley of the shadow of death, I fear no evil, for You are with me." Psalm 23:4

HOW JESUS DIED:

One of the greatest challenges that we face is dying. The Scriptures say that "it is appointed for men to die once and after this comes judgment" (Hebrews 9:27). Dying is something that the world faces with fear and dread. Yet the child of God can anticipate death without this fear or dread, trusting in the Father as Jesus did.

We know from Luke 18:31-33 that Jesus knew beforehand that he would die a horrible death. "Then He took the twelve aside and said to them, 'Behold, we are going up to Jerusalem, and all things which are written through the prophets about the Son of Man will be accomplished. [32] For He will be handed over to the Gentiles, and will be mocked and mistreated and spit upon, [33] and after they have scourged Him, they will kill Him; and the third day He will rise again.'" In Ecclesiastes 1:18, Solomon says, "Because in much wisdom there is much grief, and increasing knowledge results in increasing pain." Jesus was not blind to what He would suffer, but even with this full knowledge, He was willing to endure it for us.

Think of how honorably He hung there on the cross. 1 Peter 2:23 says, "While being reviled, He did not revile in return; while suffering, He uttered no threats, but kept entrusting Himself to Him who judges righteously." Many innocents would have railed at the soldiers: "I do not deserve to be here. I've done nothing wrong. I'm innocent." Our Lord suffered the most unjust death in history, yet His thoughts were for mankind: "Father, forgive them."

36

From His experiences in the garden, we know this horrible death that He faced was a challenge to Him, so how did He die so honorably? Again, according to 1 Peter 2:23, He "kept entrusting Himself to Him who judges righteously." Jesus "kept entrusting" Himself to the Father. This is the key.

As we read the accounts of Jesus on the cross, we realize that not only did He teach us how to live, but He also taught us how to die. They can be found in Matthew 27:27-44; Mark 15:16-32; Luke 23:26-43; and John 19:16-27.

HYMN

Nailed to the Cross (C. Breck (1899) Public Domain

There was One who was willing to die in my stead,
That a soul so unworthy might live,
And the path to the cross He was willing to tread,
All the sins of my life to forgive.

Refrain: They are nailed to the cross,
They are nailed to the cross,
O how much He was willing to bear!
With what anguish and loss,
Jesus went to the cross!
But He carried my sins with Him there.

HOW WE CAN FACE DEATH:

If the Lord does not return before our deaths, we will die. It is inevitable. Jesus is our perfect example of how to die with courage. In Gethsemane He showed us that He dreaded the experience to come, but He went through that horrible experience because He loved us and trusted God. Do we trust Him the same way?

We do not have to fear death the way the world fears it if we are following God's will. In fact, it can be a glorious experience to anticipate. Our death—the ending of our physical life—can mean that our struggle is ended, and our battle is won. Death, for a Christian, brings permanent freedom from evil. We get to go to be with the Father. Why had we rather stay here and deal with the pain and heartaches of old age? In 2 Corinthians 5:8, Paul says, "We are of good courage, I say, and prefer rather to be absent from the body and to be at home with the Lord." Let us strive to set our minds on seeking to go home to be with the Lord.

When Lazarus died, Jesus said to his sister, Martha, "'I am the resurrection and the life; he who believes in Me will live even if he dies, [26] and everyone who lives and believes in Me will never die. Do you believe this?' [27] She said to Him, 'Yes, Lord; I have believed that You are the Christ, the Son of God, even He who comes into the world.'" (John 11:25-27). Do we believe like Martha?

Can we approach death like Jesus, "entrusting Himself to Him who judges righteously," or like the apostle Paul? In 2 Timothy 4:6-8, near the end of his life, he wrote, "For I am already being poured out as a drink offering, and the time of my departure has come. [7] I have fought the good fight, I have finished the course, I have kept the faith; [8] in the future there is laid up for me the crown of righteousness, which the Lord, the righteous Judge, will award to me on that day; and not only to me, but also to all who have loved His appearing."

And remember the beloved words of David from Psalm 23:4: "Even though I walk through the valley of the shadow of death, I fear no evil, for You are with me."

38

What awaits us after death? Eternal life with the Father for all the faithful. "And the testimony is this, that God has given us eternal life, and this life is in His Son. [12] He who has the Son has the life; he who does not have the Son of God does not have the life. [13] These things I have written to you who believe in the name of the Son of God, so that you may know that you have eternal life" (1 John 5:11-13). "That you may know."

Just prior to His crucifixion, Jesus told His disciples that He would be leaving them and that they could not go with Him (John 13:33). When Peter asked where He was going, Jesus assured them that they would follow Him eventually (John 13:36-37). Do we not want to go and be with the Lord?

Just as Jesus prepared his disciples, so we should prepare our families for our departure from this life to our true home. From their youth, let us teach our children these principles: we are temporary residents on earth whose true home is in heaven (1 Peter 2:11; Hebrews 11:16), where "He has prepared a city." "For our citizenship is in heaven, from which also we eagerly wait for a Savior, the Lord Jesus Christ" (Philippians 3:20).

For Further Study: Why are we so afraid of dying? Is it because we are afraid that we are not ready for judgment? We can change that now. Is it because we do not trust His forgiveness? Find scriptures that encourage us to more diligent service and stronger trust. Many songs describe heaven, our eternal abode. Make a list of those songs that encourage you.

ENCOURAGE

"Be strong and let your heart take courage, All you who hope in the Lord." Psalm 31:24

HOW JESUS ENCOURAGES:

Jesus is the great encourager, able to make the weak strong, to anchor the soul of the hopeless, to mend the broken-hearted, and to reassure the doubting. Jesus longs to do this, yet He will not impose Himself on us. He will not force us to accept what He offers. We must reach out for His outstretched, caring hand.

More than once, Jesus assured his disciples not to be troubled. As He prepared them for His departure, He said, "Do not let your heart be troubled; believe in God, believe also in Me" (John 14:1). Then He assured them that they would come where He was going. He continues later in that same chapter, "Peace I leave with you; My peace I give to you; not as the world gives do I give to you. Do not let your heart be troubled, nor let it be fearful" (John 14:27).

In our lives, trouble will come, but do we understand that God wants us to live a worry-free life in spite of the troubles? Two encouragements about worry are recorded in Matthew 6. Referring to the care that the birds of the air and the lilies of the field receive, Jesus said, "For this reason I say to you, do not be worried about your life, as to what you will eat or what you will drink; nor for your body, as to what you will put on. Is not life more than food, and the body more than clothing?" (Verse 25). Then, He instructed, "But seek first His kingdom and His righteousness, and all these things will be added to you. So do not worry about tomorrow; for tomorrow will care for itself. Each day has enough trouble of its own" (Verses 33-34). This is how Jesus encourages.

Let these words give us encouragement today:

2 Thessalonians 2:16-17 "Now may our Lord Jesus Christ Himself and God our Father, who has loved us and given us eternal comfort and good hope by grace, [17] comfort and strengthen your hearts in every good work and word."

Philippians 4:6-7 "Be anxious for nothing, but in everything by prayer and supplication with thanksgiving let your requests be made known to God. [7] And the peace of God, which surpasses all comprehension, will guard your hearts and your minds in Christ Jesus."

Romans 15:13 "Now may the God of hope fill you with all joy and peace in believing, so that you will abound in hope by the power of the Holy Spirit."

Isaiah 40:31 "Yet those who wait for the Lord Will gain new strength; They will mount up with wings like eagles, They will run and not get tired, They will walk and not become weary."

Psalm 31:24 "Be strong and let your heart take courage, All you who hope in the Lord."

Romans 8:31-32 "What then shall we say to these things? If God is for us, who is against us? [32] He who did not spare His own Son, but delivered Him over for us all, how will He not also with Him freely give us all things?"

2 Corinthians 4:16-17 "Therefore we do not lose heart, but though our outer man is decaying, yet our inner man is being renewed day by day. [17] For momentary, light affliction is producing for us an eternal weight of glory far beyond all comparison."

HOW WE ENCOURAGE:

We all need encouragement. God, who made us, knows that and provides it. We get encouragement through the word and also the church as we encourage one another. Maybe the best way to *be* encouraged is to encourage others. Does it give us joy to think that we can encourage others? Remember what we said at the beginning of this lesson that Jesus can do—make the weak strong, anchor the soul of the hopeless, mend the broken hearted, and reassure the doubting. We can also do this for one another. Let us look at some scriptures that affirm that.

Hebrews 3:13 "But encourage one another day after day, as long as it is still called "Today,'" so that none of you will be hardened by the deceitfulness of sin."

1 Thessalonians 5:9-11, 14 "For God has not destined us for wrath, but for obtaining salvation through our Lord Jesus Christ, [10] who died for us, so that whether we are awake or asleep, we will live together with Him. [11] Therefore encourage one another and build up one another, just as you also are doing…" [14] "We urge you, brethren, admonish the unruly, encourage the fainthearted, help the weak, be patient with everyone."

Acts 20:1-2 "After the uproar had ceased, Paul sent for the disciples, and when he had exhorted them and taken his leave of them, he left to go to Macedonia. [2] When he had gone through those districts and had given them much exhortation, he came to Greece."

When we are with our brethren, do we look for words of encouragement to offer them? "And let us consider how to stimulate one another to love and good deeds, [25]not forsaking our own assembling together, as is the habit of some, but encouraging one another; and all the more as you see the day drawing near" (Hebrews 10:24-25).

For Further Study: Who can we encourage this week: the elderly, children, or weak brethren? Remember Proverbs 25:11: "Like apples of gold in settings of silver is a word spoken in right circumstances." Let us not let the week go by without encouraging someone.

HYMN

O, The Things We May Do, L. DeArmond (1916) Public Domain)

Have you lifted a stone from your brother's way,
As he struggled along life's road?
Have you lovingly touched some frail, toil worn hand,
Shared with someone his heavy load?

Refrain: O, the things we may do, you and I, you and I;
O, the love we can give if we try;
Just a word or a song as we're passing along,
They will count in the great by and by.

Have you spoken a word full of hope and cheer?
Have you walked with a slower pace,
Till the weary of heart who were stumbling on,
Took new courage to run the race? [Refrain]

Have you held up your light thro' the shadows dark,
So that somebody else might see?
Have you lived with the Christ thro' the long, long day,
Gaining many a victory? [Refrain]

BE FAITHFUL

"Well done, good and faithful slave." Matthew 2:21

HOW JESUS WAS FAITHFUL:

Faithful is defined as "worthy of trust, one that can be relied on, truthful." Countless passages tell us that God is faithful. For instance, Deuteronomy 7:9 says, "Know therefore that the LORD your God, He is God, the faithful God, who keeps His covenant and His lovingkindness to a thousandth generation with those who love Him and keep His commandments." Psalms 100:5 says, "For the LORD is good; His lovingkindness is everlasting And His faithfulness to all generations."

1 John 1:9 says, "If we confess our sins, He is faithful and righteous to forgive us our sins and to cleanse us from all unrighteousness." We do not have to worry about God keeping His promises; He is completely faithful. James 1:5 says, "But if any of you lacks wisdom, let him ask of God, who gives to all generously without reproach, and it will be given to you." Do we believe that promise?

In 1 Samuel 2:35, God promises a "faithful priest." "But I will raise up for Myself a faithful priest who will do according to what is in My heart and in My soul; and I will build him an enduring house, and he will walk before My anointed always." Jesus is that faithful high priest. Because of His faithfulness, He was able to offer the sacrifice for the sins of the world. If He had not lived a perfect life, He would not have been qualified to offer up the sacrifice. Praise be to God.

In Hebrews 3:1-2, the writer says, "Therefore, holy brethren, partakers of a heavenly calling, consider Jesus, the Apostle and High Priest of our confession; [2]He was faithful to Him who appointed Him, as Moses also was in all His house." His point is that Jesus surpassed Moses in "faithfulness." Moses endured much for the Israelites, and Jesus did even more for all of mankind.

HYMN

Great Is Thy Faithfulness T. Chisholm (1923) Public Domain

Great is thy faithfulness, O God my Father,
There is no shadow of turning with thee.
Thou changest not, thy compassions, they fail not;
As thou hast been, thou forever wilt be.

Refrain: Great is thy faithfulness!
Great is thy faithfulness!
Morning by morning new mercies I see;
All I have needed thy hand hath provided.
Great is thy faithfulness, Lord, unto me!

Summer and winter and springtime and harvest,
Sun, moon, and stars in their courses above
Join with all nature in manifold witness
To thy great faithfulness, mercy, and love. [Refrain]

Pardon for sin and a peace that endureth,
Thine own dear presence to cheer and to guide,
Strength for today and bright hope for tomorrow,
Blessings all mine, with ten thousand beside! [Refrain]

How We are Faithful:

Jesus said to the church in Smyrna, "Do not fear what you are about to suffer. Behold, the devil is about to cast some of you into prison, so that you will be tested, and you will have tribulation for ten days. Be faithful until [*unto*, KJV] death, and I will give you the crown of life" (Revelation 2:10). Be faithful even to the point of death.

That is our challenge. In other words, be faithful today and every day until our death and even if it requires our death. But it starts today, not tomorrow. On the day we read these words, be faithful that day.

Even in perilous times, many were faithful. To those in Ephesus and Colossae, Paul addressed the "faithful" in Christ Jesus Some were called faithful by name: Epaphras (Colossians 1:7), Tychicus (4:7), Onesimus (4:9), Silvanus (1 Peter 5:12). Wouldn't those be sweet words if they described us? Faithful David? Faithful Cynthia? Faithful _____? (Put your name here).

What does it mean to be faithful? Jesus told a parable of faithful and unfaithful servants (Matthew 25:14-30). "For it is just like a man about to go on a journey, who called his own slaves and entrusted his possessions to them" (Verse 14). Even though we call this the "Parable of the Talents," it is not about using our talents (capabilities), per se. The talent was an amount of money, which the NIV renders "bags of gold." The fundamental meaning of the parable is how faithfully the servants cared for His possessions while the master was away. Read the parable without the word "talents" to get a clearer meaning.

The master clearly represents Jesus, who was going away. The servants are His disciples. The bags of gold represent the work that the Lord left His disciples to do – teach the word to the lost to plant the kingdom of heaven in people's hearts (Luke 8:11). He gave them their bags of gold when He said, "Go and make disciples," when He told them to let their lights shine before men to glorify the Father, and when He told them to be the salt of the earth and a city on a hill, etc. He did not expect more of them than they were able to do, but to do "according to their abilities." Why did the unfaithful servant fail? He said he was afraid of displeasing the master because he was a "hard" man. According to Vine's Dictionary this means harsh. But look at the master's treatment of the other two servants. Was He really harsh? With all three servants he was fair in his treatment, but He expected faithful service.

So how faithful are we to the service Jesus left us to do? Do we learn and teach His word? Do we serve others in kindness? Do we encourage the fainthearted and raise up the fallen? Do we devote time every day to the Lord? Do we seek to grow in His grace and truth? Do we pray to be more faithful? How will our faithfulness be judged?

For Further Study: "Be faithful until death, and I will give you the crown of life" (Revelation 2:10). When the Lord returns, we will be judged on our faithfulness. This is the theme of the entire chapter of Matthew 25. The Parable of the Virgins: we must be prepared for His return. The Parable of the Bags of Gold: we must be faithful in our service. The Judgement Scene: we must be ready for judgement. Study Matthew 25 again. Let us resolve to greater faithfulness.

FINISH

"Let us not lose heart in doing good, for in due time we will reap if we do not grow weary." Galatians 6:9

HOW JESUS FINISHED:

Just after Jesus, hanging on the cross, had given instructions to John on the care of his mother, "Jesus, knowing that all things had already been accomplished, to fulfill the Scripture, said, 'I am thirsty.' 29 A jar full of sour wine was standing there; so they put a sponge full of the sour wine upon a branch of hyssop and brought it up to His mouth. 30 Therefore when Jesus had received the sour wine, He said, "It is finished!" And He bowed His head and gave up His spirit" (John 19:28-30).

"It is finished" was the last thing Jesus said before dying. Found only in John 19:30, the word "finished" here comes from the Greek word *teleo* meaning "bringing to an end, completing, accomplishing." Translators say that this word signifies the successful end to a particular course of action. It is the word you would use when you finish a marathon, make the final payment on your house, or complete some other great accomplishment. You are not just done, you have finished! It is the same word translated "accomplished" immediately preceding this in verse 28. It says Jesus knew that all things had been accomplished, so He could say, "It is finished."

When Jesus said, "It is finished," it was not the whisper of a worn-out, defeated, and dying man. It was a victorious proclamation. He had done all that He needed to do to make God known to men and to show His love to man. In John 17:4, He prayed, "I glorified You on the earth, having accomplished the work which You have given Me to do." On the cross, He paid the

48

full and total price of our redemption. That is the power of "It is finished."

Think of what it had taken for Jesus to finish and what He went through to finish. He did not give up when he was ridiculed or beaten. He did not give in when the devil tempted Him or when He was scourged and put on the cross. He finished, for the Father and for us. He victoriously finished.

We cannot say often enough that Jesus left heaven and came to earth to do the will of the Father. Early in His ministry, Jesus said to His disciples, "'My food is to do the will of Him who sent me and to accomplish his work'" (John 4:34). Food is what sustains you. Doing the will of the Father and finishing His work was what sustained Jesus from the outset to the end. With "It is finished," Jesus signified the completion of His purpose for coming to earth. He had fulfilled all the Old Testament prophecies, symbols, and foreshadowing about Himself. Jesus' perfect life of obedience was now complete.

➢ The decisive battle with the enemy was won. It is finished.
➢ The debt of sin was paid. It is finished.
➢ Man's atoning sacrifice was offered. It is finished.

We could say the greatest accomplishment of all history was finished. Praise God; it is finished.

HOW WE FINISH:

Paul used the same Greek word *teleo* in 2 Timothy 4:6-7 when he wrote that he had "finished the course." "For I am now ready to be offered, and the time of my departure is at hand. I have fought a good fight, I have finished the course, I have kept the faith" (Verse 7).

He also used it in that touching farewell meeting with the Ephesian elders. He said to them, "However, I consider my life worth nothing to me; my only aim is to finish the race and complete the task the Lord Jesus has given me—the task of testifying to the good news of God's grace" (Acts 20:24 NIV).

With these words, the Holy Spirit through Paul exhorts *us* to finish: "Let us not lose heart in doing good, for in due time we will reap if we do not grow weary" (Galatians 6:9). How many have you known that started, but did not finish, who grew weary and gave up? Consider these other exhortations to "finish."

Hebrews 12:2-3: "Fixing our eyes on Jesus, the author and perfecter of faith, who for the joy set before Him endured the cross, despising the shame, and has sat down at the right hand of the throne of God.³ For consider Him who has endured such hostility by sinners against Himself, so that you will not grow weary and lose heart." Think of what Jesus did for us and finish.

Philippians 3:12, 14: "Not that I have already obtained it or have already become perfect, but I press on so that I may lay hold of that for which also was laid hold of by Christ Jesus... ¹⁴ I press on toward the goal for the prize of the upward call of God in Christ Jesus." Press on and finish.

Like Jesus, we must finish. In our wedding ceremony, we make a promise to never give up: "Till death do us part." Make that same commitment, that same vow, to God: "I will never give up on You. I will be faithful unto death." Every morning, make the commitment, "I will devote today to Your service. I will finish today." Then, when we reach the end of our life's journey, we can say, "It is finished."

For Further Study Read more scriptures about persevering to the end. Let us pray often to remain steadfast, for we know that our labor is not in vain, not if we finish.

HYMN

Hallelujah! What a Savior! P.P. Bliss (1875) Public Domain

"Man of Sorrows!" what a name
For the Son of God, who came
Ruined sinners to reclaim. Hallelujah! What a Savior!

Bearing shame and scoffing rude,
In my place condemned He stood;
Sealed my pardon with His blood. Hallelujah! What a Savior!

Guilty, vile, and helpless we;
Spotless Lamb of God was He;
"Full atonement!" can it be? Hallelujah! What a Savior!

Lifted up was He to die;
"It is finished!" was His cry;
Now in Heav'n exalted high. Hallelujah! What a Savior

When He comes, our glorious King,
All His ransomed home to bring,
Then anew His song we'll sing: Hallelujah! What a Savior!

FORGIVE

"Be kind to one another, tender-hearted, forgiving each other, just as God in Christ also has forgiven you." Ephesians 4:32

HOW JESUS FORGIVES:

When Jesus was still hanging on the cross, He uttered those precious words: "Father, forgive them; for they do not know what they are doing" (Luke 23:34). The literal meaning of the Greek word translated "forgive" here is "to let go, give up a debt, to remit." What does this forgiveness mean to us? Every person that has ever lived is in need of forgiveness from God because Romans 3:23 says that all have incurred the debt of sin and come short of the glory of God. The punishment for sin is spiritual death, separation from God. But because of His love, God provided a way for us to be brought back to Him. A sacrifice would be made for our sins. "And He Himself bore our sins in His body on the cross, so that we might die to sin and live to righteousness; for by His wounds you were healed" (1 Peter 2:24). That is how Jesus forgives.

For our forgiveness, Christ died for us even though we were sinners and enemies of God. "For while we were still helpless, at the right time Christ died for the ungodly. [7] For one will hardly die for a righteous man; though perhaps for the good man someone would dare even to die. [8] But God demonstrates His own love toward us, in that while we were yet sinners, Christ died for us. [9] Much more then, having now been justified by His blood, we shall be saved from the wrath of God through Him. [10] For if while we were enemies we were reconciled to God through the death of His Son, much more, having been reconciled, we shall be saved by His life" (Romans 5:6-10). That is how Jesus forgives.

We cannot talk about how Jesus forgives without talking about love, because love is the motivation for His forgiveness. John 3:16 says that love motivated the giving of the Son. 1 John 4:9-10 expounds on that thought. "By this the love of God was manifested in us, that God has sent His only begotten Son into the world so that we might live through Him. [10] In this is love, not that we loved God, but that He loved us and sent His Son to be the propitiation [satisfaction] for our sins." Because of love is why Jesus forgives.

Romans 6:23 portrays a stark contrast between sin leading to death and God's free gift of eternal life. "For the wages of sin is death, but the free gift of God is eternal life in Christ Jesus our Lord." That gift of eternal life is only in Christ Jesus our Lord. So how do we get into Christ? How do we access this forgiveness of our sins that is found in Him?

Paul told the Roman brethren in Romans 6:3, "Or do you not know that all of us who have been baptized into Christ Jesus have been baptized into His death?" To the Galatians he wrote in Galatians 3:27: "For all of you who were baptized into Christ have clothed yourselves with Christ." Peter told those on Pentecost who believed his message about Jesus, "Repent, and each of you be baptized in the name of Jesus Christ for the forgiveness of your sins; and you will receive the gift of the Holy Spirit" (Acts 2:38). The way to get into Christ, where forgiveness is found, is to believe on Him as the Son of God and be obedient to Him in baptism. Thank God for His forgiveness in Christ Jesus our Lord.

HOW WE FORGIVE:

We often say that God has prescribed the very best way to live, and His prescription to forgive is a perfect example. Even secular mental health professionals say that it is healthy to forgive, that holding on to anger, resentment and thoughts of revenge can fill us with bitterness towards life. So then, not only is forgiveness a gift that we give others but a gift to ourselves also.

Matthew 18:23-35 relates Jesus' mighty parable of forgiveness. "For this reason the kingdom of heaven may be compared to a king who wished to settle accounts with his slaves. [24] When he had begun to settle them, one who owed him ten thousand talents was brought to him. [25] But since he did not have the means to repay, his lord commanded him to be sold, along with his wife and children and all that he had, and repayment to be made. [26] So the slave fell to the ground and prostrated himself before him, saying, 'Have patience with me and I will repay you everything.' [27] And the lord of that slave felt compassion and released him and forgave him the debt.

[28] But that slave went out and found one of his fellow slaves who owed him a hundred denarii; and he seized him and began to choke him, saying, 'Pay back what you owe.' [29] So his fellow slave fell to the ground and began to plead with him, saying, 'Have patience with me and I will repay you.' [30] But he was unwilling and went and threw him in prison until he should pay back what was owed. [31] So when his fellow slaves saw what had happened, they were deeply grieved and came and reported to their lord all that had happened. [32] Then summoning him, his lord said to him, 'You wicked slave, I forgave you all that debt because you pleaded with me. [33] Should you not also have had mercy on your fellow slave, in the same way that I had mercy on you?'

[34]And his lord, moved with anger, handed him over to the torturers until he should repay all that was owed him. [35] My heavenly Father will also do the same to you, if each of you does not forgive his brother from your heart."

Does God's gracious forgiveness motivate us to forgive others? Jesus warned us that it must, as He said, "But if you do not forgive others, then your Father will not forgive your transgressions" (Matthew 6:15). And Paul emphasizes that we must follow the example of God in Christ. "Be kind to one another, tender-hearted, forgiving each other, just as God in Christ also has forgiven you" (Ephesians 4:32).

Other verses on forgiveness:

Colossians 3:13 "Bearing with one another, and forgiving each other, whoever has a complaint against anyone; just as the Lord forgave you, so also should you."

Matthew 18:21-22 "Then Peter came and said to Him, 'Lord, how often shall my brother sin against me and I forgive him? Up to seven times?' Jesus said to him, 'I do not say to you, up to seven times, but up to seventy times seven.'"

A common question about forgiveness is: Must Christians forgive someone who has wronged us if they will not repent and ask our forgiveness? We know that God requires repentance, so should we also? In Luke 17:3-4, Jesus says, "If your brother sins, rebuke him, and if he repents, forgive him, and if he sins against you seven times in the day, and turns to you seven times, saying, 'I repent,' you must forgive him." Jesus is not referring to hurt feelings or a slight of some sort. He is talking about a sin against you – lying, cheating, stealing, i.e., something that would stand between the sinner and God. It is our responsibility to help the sinner to repent to save his soul. On the other hand, it does not mean that we harbor ill feelings. We must pray for them, return good for evil, and treat them with love (Matthew 5:43-44).

For Further Study: Find more examples of forgiveness in the Scriptures. Do a word study of "forgive". What is the first instance where the word occurs? Let us search our hearts. Are there those that we need to forgive? Pray to God about forgiving them.

BE A FRIEND

"You are My friends if you do what I command you." John 15:14

HOW JESUS IS A FRIEND:

Friendship can be described as a relationship of trust, honesty, fellowship, enjoyment, and love. *Philos* is the Greek word translated "friend" in the New Testament. You can see it is related to *phileō* which means brotherly love.

As Jesus walked on earth, he developed close friendships with others. Jesus called Lazarus *philos* in John 11:11. We know He loved (*agapē*) all people and that He came to seek and save all, but there were those with whom Jesus had a special, close relationship. Can you imagine how it would affect you for Jesus to call you his true friend? It also seems a bit ironic that one of the charges that the Jews made against Jesus was that he was a friend of tax collectors and sinners (Matthew 11:19).

As Jesus was preparing his disciples for his departure, He talked to them about love and friendship. "Greater love has no one than this, that one lay down his life for his friends. [14] You are My friends if you do what I command you. [15] No longer do I call you slaves, for the slave does not know what his master is doing, but I have called you friends, for all things that I have heard from My Father I have made known to you" (John 15:13-14).

What about us? Is Jesus a friend to us? Notice verse 13 above. Jesus showed His friendship to us by dying for us to save us from our sins. No one could love us more than that, and no one could be a better friend than Jesus. Think of the old, old song that we used to sing so often: *What a friend we have in Jesus* (Joseph

Scriven, 1855). "What a Friend we have in Jesus, all our sins and griefs to bear! What a privilege to carry everything to God in prayer!" Another line says, "Can we find a friend so faithful who will all our sorrows share? Jesus knows our every weakness; take it to the Lord in prayer." We thank Jesus for His friendship.

HOW WE ARE FRIENDS:

In John 15:14, Jesus tells us how we can be His friend: if we do what He commands. In James 2:23, Abraham is called the friend of God: "And the Scripture was fulfilled which says, 'And Abraham believed God, and it was accounted to him for righteousness.' And he was called the friend of God." Notice how similar this is to John 15:14. Abraham believed (trusted) God enough that when God told him to sacrifice Isaac, he immediately set out to obey (Genesis 22). The result of such obedience, predicated on faith, was that he was called the friend of God. Let us commit ourselves to being God's friend by trusting and obeying Him. Think of the joy we receive to know God views us as His friend. We think it is an honor to have a renowned person as a friend, but this is the one and only true God.

One of the deepest human friendships described in the Bible began in 1 Samuel 18:1-5 with the first meeting of Jonathan and David. Upon their meeting, it is said the "soul of Jonathan was knit to the soul of David, and Jonathan loved him as himself." Right then they made a covenant, a solemn agreement, that bound them together as life-long friends. Jonathan and David shared a solid basis for their friendship: a strong faith and deep love for Jehovah. David never forgot his vow to Jonathan, and years later, long after Jonathan's death, he sought out and took care of Jonathan's disabled son, Mephibosheth (2 Samuel 9:1-13).

Just as friendship was important to David, it is important to us. Friends should be chosen carefully because, as Paul told the Corinthians, bad company corrupts good morals (1 Corinthians 15:33). On the other hand, if we choose friends wisely, friendship can strengthen our faith. As Ecclesiastes 4:9-10 says, "Two are better than one because they have a good return for their labor. [10] For if either of them falls, the one will lift up his companion. But woe to the one who falls when there is not another to lift him up." There is no more valuable gift that we can give our friends than to lift them up spiritually.

And we must allow friends to lift us up, even if it might be "tough love." Remember the Scripture: "So have I become your enemy by telling you the truth?" (Galatians 4:16). Paul reminded the Galatians how positively they had at one time received him and his message. But they had changed. He said that at one time "if possible, you would have plucked out your eyes and given them to me" (Verse 15), but Judaizing teachers had moved in to convince them that Paul and his teachings were not true. Their rejection of the gospel had deeply hurt him. Do we reject friendship if our friend dares to tell us a hard truth?

Truth can sometimes be hard to hear. Proverbs 27:6 says, "Faithful are the wounds of a friend, But deceitful are the kisses of an enemy." Real friends tell us the truth, even if it hurts and even if it risks the friendship. They tell the truth in love so we can grow from it (Proverbs 9:8-9; Proverbs 27:17). Who were the true friends, the apostle Paul or the Judaizers?

In Mark 5:18-19 we learn of a man that Jesus had healed of demons who begged to go with Jesus. He did not permit it, but instead said to him, "Go home to your friends, and tell them what great things the Lord has done for you, and how He has had compassion on you" (NKJV). Jesus could say this to us. Tell your friends how much the Lord has done for you and how he has had mercy on you. True friendship shares our faith with our friends.

For Further Study Thought question: What do you do if a friend betrays you? What does Jesus do when we betray Him?

HYMN

I'll Be a Friend to Jesus J. Oatman, Jr. (1922) Public Domain

They tried my Lord and Master, With no one to defend;
Within the halls of Pilate He stood without a friend.

Refrain: I'll be a friend to Jesus, My life for Him I'll spend;
I'll be a friend to Jesus, Until my years shall end.

The world may turn against Him, I'll love Him to the end,
And while on earth I'm living, My Lord shall have a friend.
[Refrain]

I'll do what He may bid me; I'll go where He may send;
I'll try each flying moment To prove that I'm His friend. [Refrain]

To all who need a Savior, My Friend I'll recommend;
Because He brought salvation, Is why I am His friend. [Refrain]

BE GENTLE

"Brethren, even if anyone is caught in any trespass, you who are spiritual, restore such a one in a spirit of gentleness" Galatians 6:1

HOW JESUS IS GENTLE:

Gentle is defined as having a mild or tender temperament or character, moderate in action, effect, or degree, not harsh or severe. Gentleness is controlled strength. Think of physical situations that call for gentleness: holding a newborn baby, for instance. Yet that is also where the strength comes in; you would not want someone that is feeble holding a baby.

Jesus describes himself as gentle when he beckons the weary and burdened to come to Him. We sometimes get caught up with the rebukes of Jesus for the Jewish leaders of the day and neglect the images of the gentleness of Jesus as he went among the people. To the people He said, "Come to Me, all who are weary and heavy-laden, and I will give you rest. [29]Take My yoke upon you and learn from Me, for I am gentle and humble in heart, and you will find rest for your souls" (Matthew 11:28-29). He uses a metaphor of a farmer yoking animals to control and guide them. When we allow Jesus to put His yoke on us, we are giving Him control over our lives. He is gentle and humble in His treatment of us, as a farmer might gently work his obedient animals.

In Isaiah 42:3, Isaiah illustrates the gentleness of the Messiah. "A bruised reed He will not break, And a dimly burning wick He will not extinguish." If we are bruised, Jesus will handle us so gently that He will not break us. If we are a "dimly burning wick," rather than snuff us out, he will reignite us. Imagine someone over a fire gently blowing on a smoking wick to get it to flame. That is how Jesus handles us in gentleness.

The hymn *Lead me Gently Home* (Will L. Thompson) talks about our road from here to heaven. Imagine holding the Lord's hand as He keeps our feet from wandering off the road. Isaiah 41:13 says, "For I am the LORD your God, who upholds your right hand, Who says to you, 'Do not fear, I will help you.'" Thank you, Father, for your gentle guidance.

HYMN

Lead Me Gently Home W. Thompson (1879) Public Domain

Lead me gently home, Father, Lead me gently home,
When life's toils are ended And parting days have come;
Sin no more shall tempt me, Ne'er from Thee I'll roam,
If Thou'lt only lead me,
Father, Lead me gently home.

Refrain: Lead me gently home, Father
Lead me gently home, Father,
Lest I fall upon the wayside,
Lead me gently home.

Lead me gently home, Father, Lead me gently home,
In life's darkest hours, Father, When life's troubles come;
Keep my feet from wand'ring, Lest from Thee I roam,
Lest I fall upon the wayside,
Lead me gently home. Refrain

HOW WE ARE TO BE GENTLE:

If we love the image of the Lord holding our hand, then think of us reaching a hand gently to those who need us. This is the idea of Galatians 6:1. "Brethren, even if anyone is caught in any trespass, you who are spiritual, restore such a one in a spirit of gentleness; each one looking to yourself, so that you too will not be tempted." Again, think of the infant that needs our strong, yet gentle touch. Do we emphasize this aspect enough as we work to save those in sin? Paul described it this way, "But we proved to be gentle among you, as a nursing mother tenderly cares for her own children" (1 Thessalonians 2:7).

Vine's describes the Greek word *epieikēs* that is translated "gentleness" as "equitable, fair, moderate, forbearing." And it says that it "expresses that considerateness that looks humanely and reasonably at the facts of a case." In 2 Timothy 2:25 Paul again emphasizes this gentle restoration: "With gentleness correcting those who are in opposition, if perhaps God may grant them repentance leading to the knowledge of the truth." And to Titus, he says to remind believers "to malign no one, to be peaceable, gentle, showing every consideration for all men." And then says in the next verse, "For we also once were foolish ourselves, disobedient, deceived, enslaved to various lusts and pleasures, spending our life in malice and envy, hateful, hating one another" (Titus 3:2-3). Since we were once sinners, we have no justification for anything but gentleness when dealing with the erring. "There but for the grace of God go I."

The wise man of Proverbs contrasts gentle words with harsh ones: "A gentle answer turns away wrath, But a harsh word stirs up anger. ² The tongue of the wise makes knowledge acceptable, But the mouth of fools spouts folly" (Proverbs 15:1-2).

James shows that gentleness comes from the wisdom from above. "Who among you is wise and understanding? Let him show by his good behavior his deeds in the gentleness of wisdom" (James 3:13). "But the wisdom from above is first pure, then peaceable, gentle, reasonable, full of mercy and good fruits, unwavering, without hypocrisy" (James 3:17).

The New Testament is full of exhortations for us to be gentle. Notice that gentleness is one of the results or outcomes of being led by the Spirit. "But the fruit of the Spirit is love, joy, peace, patience, kindness, goodness, faithfulness, [23] gentleness, self-control; against such things there is no law" (Galatians 5:22-23).

It is an aspect of the manner of walk that is "worthy" or fitting to our calling. "Therefore I, the prisoner of the Lord, implore you to walk in a manner worthy of the calling with which you have been called, [2] with all humility and gentleness, with patience, showing tolerance for one another in love" (Ephesians 4:12).

Our gentleness should be so obvious that it is known by all. "Let your gentle spirit be known to all men. The Lord is near" (Philippians 4:5).

So there is no doubt that we are to be gentle with one another as we walk hand in hand with the Father and with one another towards heaven. We have the example of a gentle Master who leads us with a light yoke. He handles us like a bruised reed that He doesn't want to break. Thank God for His gentleness and let us emulate it.

For Further Study: Find other passages that deal with gentleness Do a self-evaluation. Are we gentle when working with the weak?

GIVE

"They first gave themselves to the Lord and to us by the will of God." 2 Corinthians 8:5

HOW JESUS GIVES:

Jesus gave His all. In Matthew 20:28, He says that he came "to give his life a ransom for many." A ransom is the price that has to be paid for a life. We know it best as the price to buy back someone who has been kidnapped. 1 Corinthians 6:20 says, "For you have been bought with a price." The ransom price was the life and death of Jesus. How could we ask more?

The Spirit reveals in Romans 6:23: "For the wages of sin is death, but the free gift of God is eternal life in Christ Jesus our Lord." And in Ephesians 2:8: "For by grace you have been saved through faith; and that not of yourselves, it is the gift of God." One of the most beloved scriptures speaks of how the Father gave. "For God so loved the world, that He gave His only begotten Son, that whoever believes in Him shall not perish, but have eternal life" (John 3:16). God's gift is motivated by His love for us.

In his first epistle, John says, "See how great a love the Father has bestowed on us, that we would be called children of God; and such we are" (1 John 3:1). One translation says God has "lavished" us with love. This speaks to the relationship that we have with God through Christ. Do we appreciate and humbly thank God for His great gift? In fact, James says that every good gift comes from God. "Every good thing given and every perfect gift is from above, coming down from the Father of lights" (James 1:17). Let us examine our hearts to see how we appreciate gifts from the Father.

We strive all our lives for the gift Jesus gives to the faithful. After warning the Smyrna church of persecutions to come, He said, "Be faithful until death, and I will give you the crown of life" (Revelation 2:10). The word used for "crown" is *stephanos*, which means here "the wreath given as a prize to victors in public games." James uses the same word when he says, "Blessed is a man who perseveres under trial; for once he has been approved, he will receive the crown of life which the Lord has promised to those who love Him" (James 1:12). Also see 1 Peter 5:4.

As he neared death, Paul said, "In the future there is laid up for me the crown of righteousness, which the Lord, the righteous Judge, will award to me on that day; and not only to me, but also to all who have loved His appearing" (2 Timothy 4:8). We thank the Lord for His great gifts.

HYMN

Jesus Paid it All M.S. Shaffer (1915) Public Domain

Gone is all my debt of sin, A great change is wrought within,
And to live I now begin, Risen from the fall;
Yet the debt I did not pay—Someone died for me one day,
Sweeping all the debt away—Jesus paid it all.

Refrain: Jesus died and paid it all, yes, On the cross of Calvary
And my stony heart was melted At His dying, dying call;
Oh, His heart in shame was broken On the tree for you and me,
Yes, and the debt, the debt is canceled, Jesus paid it, paid it all.

Sinner, not for me alone Did the Son of God atone;
Your debt, too, He made His own, On the cruel tree.
Come to Him with all your sin; Be as white as snow within;
Full salvation you may win And rejoice with me. Refrain

HOW WE GIVE:

God loves a cheerful giver (2 Corinthians 9:7). Let us start here, because our giving hinges on this concept. Whatever we give must come from a cheerful, willing heart. If we give a little or a lot, if it comes from a grudging heart, it does not please God. Paul tells of why the Macedonians gave so generously. "They first gave themselves to the Lord and to us by the will of God" (2 Corinthians 8:5). In his emotional meeting with the Ephesian elders, Paul reminded them to remember the words of the Lord Jesus: "It is more blessed to give than to receive" (Acts 20:35).

Who could illustrate giving oneself to the Lord better than the widow that gave her all? "And He sat down opposite the treasury and began observing how the people were putting money into the treasury; and many rich people were putting in large sums. [42] A poor widow came and put in two small copper coins, which amount to a cent. [43] Calling His disciples to Him, He said to them, 'Truly I say to you, this poor widow put in more than all the contributors to the treasury; [44] for they all put in out of their surplus, but she, out of her poverty, put in all she owned, all she had to live on.'" (Mark 12:41–44). What great dependence on God she illustrates in her generosity!

Sometimes we hear the "prosperity gospel." Central to the doctrine is the idea of giving to the church as an investment. Givers are promised a monetary return on their investment: a "hundredfold," a reference to Mark 10:30. But that is both a false interpretation of Mark 10:30 and poor motivation for giving. We need to give because God loves a generous heart. *That* is our motivation for giving. If we do not yearn to give, doesn't that mean we have not given our hearts to God?

Another bad motivation for giving is to receive recognition from others. Jesus warns about this in Matthew 6:2-4. He says, "So when you give to the poor, do not sound a trumpet before you, as the hypocrites do in the synagogues and in the streets, so that they may be honored by men. Truly I say to you, they have their reward in full." If we are giving in order to receive recognition of others, then that is all we will get.

So if we are to give like Jesus, what did Jesus give? He gave His all. How did He give? Out of His abundant love for us. That is our example.

For Further Study: Study 2 Corinthians 8:1-5. Their attitude and action in giving was a tremendous example. Why did they give? How? Let us think of ways to give with a more generous heart.

HYMN

Give Me Thy Heart E. E. Hewitt (1898) Public Domain

"Give Me thy heart," says the Father above,
No gift so precious to Him as our love;
Softly He whispers, wherever thou art,
"Gratefully trust Me, and give Me thy heart."

Refrain: "Give Me thy heart, give Me thy heart,"
Hear the soft whisper, wherever thou art:
From this dark world He would draw thee apart;
Speaking so tenderly, "Give Me thy heart."

"Give Me thy heart," says the Savior of men,
Calling in mercy again and again;
"Turn now from sin, and from evil depart,
Have I not died for thee? Give Me thy heart." Refrain

"Give Me thy heart," says the Spirit divine,
"All that thou hast, to My keeping resign;
Grace more abounding is Mine to impart,
Make full surrender and give Me thy heart." Refrain

GO HOME TO THE FATHER

"Keep seeking the things above, where Christ is,
seated at the right hand of God." Colossians 3:1

HOW JESUS WENT HOME:

Shortly before His death, Jesus said to His disciples, "I came forth from the Father and have come into the world; I am leaving the world again and going to the Father" (John 16:28). These were not new ideas to them—Jesus had already told them—but very soon they would take on an urgency like never before.

Jesus had told his disciples of going home to the Father in John 14:3, where He said, "If I go and prepare a place for you, I will come again and receive you to Myself, that where I am, there you may be also." And in John 14:28-29, He said, "You heard that I said to you, 'I go away, and I will come to you.' If you loved Me, you would have rejoiced because I go to the Father, for the Father is greater than I. [29] Now I have told you before it happens, so that when it happens, you may believe."

After Jesus said, "It is finished" on the cross, "He bowed his head and gave up his spirit" (John 19:30). His dead body remained on the cross until it was taken down and placed in a nearby tomb (John 19:38-42). Three days later, His body and spirit were reunited, and He rose from the dead (John 20). But where was His spirit for the three days between His death and resurrection?

We know that He was not in heaven because after His resurrection, Jesus told Mary that He had not yet ascended to the Father (John 20:17). Our clearest indication of where He had been comes from the cross where Jesus promised the believing thief, "Truly I say to you, today you shall be with Me in Paradise (Luke 23:43). Paradise is the place where the righteous go after death to await judgment. In his story of the rich man and Lazarus, Jesus says that Lazarus went there after he died (Luke 16:22). So, after His death, the spirit of Jesus went to Paradise to await His resurrection.

During the 40 days between His resurrection and ascension, Jesus appeared to others offering proof of his resurrection, as recorded in the gospels. Then in Acts 1: 9-11, we see the ascension back to the Father. "He was lifted up while they were looking on, and a cloud received Him out of their sight. [10] And as they were gazing intently into the sky while He was going, behold, two men in white clothing stood beside them. [11] They also said, 'Men of Galilee, why do you stand looking into the sky? This Jesus, who has been taken up from you into heaven, will come in just the same way as you have watched Him go into heaven.'" Just imagine what a sight that would have been to witness.

What a relief it must have been for Jesus to return to the Father. What a joy! It is a profound example to us. He had finished His course to save man from their sins, and now He could go home to the Father.

HOW WE WILL GO HOME:

Have you ever been truly homesick? When I (David) was in the Marines, I had to be away from home for two full years.

How deep was that pain of yearning to see my mama, daddy, and family. When the day finally arrived to go home, my daddy met me at the Nashville airport. As I got off the plane, I spotted him waiting in the door. There is no telling how long my daddy had been standing in that door, waiting to welcome his son home.

Is that not how it is going to be when we go home to the Father? If we die before the Lord returns, our spirits are taken to Paradise, the same place that Jesus went after His death, where the righteous are comforted (Luke 16:19-31). After the Lord returns, and after the resurrection and judgment, Jesus will take the saved home to the Father, all described in 1 Thessalonians 4:13-17.

We are longing for the day that the Lord will welcome us into our eternal home. In Colossians 3:1-2, Paul urges, "Therefore if you have been raised up with Christ, keep seeking the things above, where Christ is, seated at the right hand of God. [2] Set your mind on the things above, not on the things that are on earth." Let us heed the exhortation. "Keep seeking the things above" as we set our minds on things above. We are bound for the promised land!

And just as Jesus prepared the disciples for *His* leaving, He prepares us for *our* leaving. Paul assures us that when our body is torn down (death), we have another one from God, eternal in the heavens (2 Corinthians 5:1). In the eighth verse, Paul says, "We are of good courage, I say, and prefer rather to be absent from the body and to be at home with the Lord." Paul would rather be at home with the Lord than in his burdened, dying body. Paul believes that the glory of his eternal life will far outweigh the suffering of earthly life, and that is what we also should believe.

Then Paul condenses his life's goals into one single thing: to please Christ. "Therefore we also have as our ambition, whether at home or absent, to be pleasing to Him. [10] For we must all appear before the judgment seat of Christ, so that each one may be recompensed for his deeds in the body, according to what he has done, whether good or bad" (2 Corinthians 5:9-10). Whether here in difficult earthly life, or at home with Christ in glorious eternity, he wants to please Christ. That is Paul's ultimate purpose, and it is ours as well. Let us please Christ so that we can go home to the Father. Let us go home.

For Further Study: Read Philippians 1:21-23, 1 Thessalonians 4:13-18, and 1 Corinthians 15:20-28.

HYMN

This World is Not my Home, A. Carter (1931) Public Domain

This world is not my home, I'm just a passing through
My treasures are laid up somewhere beyond the blue;
The angels beckon me from heaven's open door,
And I can't feel at home in this world anymore.

Chorus: O Lord, you know I have no friend like you,
If heaven's not my home, then Lord what will I do?
The angels beckon me from heaven's open door,
And I can't feel at home in this world anymore.

They're all expecting me, and that's one thing I know,
My Savior pardoned me and now I onward go;
I know He'll take me through though I am weak and poor,
And I can't feel at home in this world anymore. [Chorus]

Just up in glory-land we'll live eternally,
The saints on every hand are shouting victory,
Their songs of sweetest praise drift back from heaven's shore,
And I can't feel at home in this world anymore. [Chorus]

GROW

"But grow in the grace and knowledge of our Lord and
Savior Jesus Christ." 2 Peter 3:18

HOW JESUS GREW:

Jesus came to earth as an infant, conceived by the Holy
Spirit, and birthed by the virgin Mary (Luke 1-2). Two places in
scripture tell us of His growth as a child. "When they had
performed everything according to the Law of the Lord, they
returned to Galilee, to their own city of Nazareth. [40] The Child
continued to grow and become strong, increasing in wisdom; and
the grace of God was upon Him" (Luke 2:39-40). "And Jesus kept
increasing in wisdom and stature, and in favor with God and men"
(Luke 2:52).

We know so little about the young person Jesus. These
two stages of growth are really all that we know, one as a very
young child and one at the age of twelve. They state that at birth
Jesus was not full grown in maturity, any more than he was
physically. Notice his four areas of growth at the age of twelve.
Mentally (wisdom), physically (stature), spiritually (favor with God),
and socially (favor with man)

Another scripture, Hebrews 5:8-9, tells us about Jesus'
growth process. "Although He was a Son, He learned obedience
from the things which He suffered. [9] And having been made
perfect, He became to all those who obey Him the source of eternal
salvation." "Learned" here carries with it the idea of experiencing or
practicing. The focus of this verse is not so much on Jesus
becoming aware of what suffering is but putting into practice what
He was called to do.

It says Jesus was made "perfect." The term "perfect," in most biblical contexts, carries the idea of completion or maturity. It is the same word that is translated "accomplished" in John 17:4: "I glorified You on the earth, having accomplished the work which You have given Me to do." Jesus moved from untested faith into temptation and suffering, and then through temptation and suffering into tested and proven obedience. He completed this without ever failing.

Hebrews 2:17-18 tells us why this is so important: "Therefore, He had to be made like His brethren in all things, so that He might become a merciful and faithful high priest in things pertaining to God, to make propitiation for the sins of the people. [18] For since He Himself was tempted in that which He has suffered, He is able to come to the aid of those who are tempted."

How blessed we are that He would do this for us. Deity could never be tempted. He had to clothe Himself with human form to experience temptation. Thanks be to God, Jesus grew from untested to tested without ever failing, making Him qualified to come to the aid of us when we are tempted. That is how Jesus grew from conception to death.

HOW WE GROW:

It is very easy to go through life either skipping along, quite satisfied, or being so burdened down with guilt that we continue to be stuck in a spiritual rut. But look how the apostle Peter talks about growth. He had just warned not to be led away by false teachers, "but grow in the grace and knowledge of our Lord and Savior Jesus Christ. To Him be the glory, both now and to the day of eternity. Amen" (2 Peter 3:18). Look at what we are to grow in: "The grace and knowledge of our Lord and Savior Jesus Christ."

Growing in the grace and knowledge of Jesus is developing our relationship with Him so that we become more and more like Him. Peter describes Jesus here as both our Lord and our Savior. We must continue to grow in our submission to Jesus as Lord and in our worship of Him as Savior. It reminds us that our goal in this study is to become like Jesus more and more every day as we walk in His footsteps. By that we will grow in His grace and knowledge.

Ephesians 4:13-15 explains how to grow up in Christ in the context of church unity. "Until we all attain to the unity of the faith, and of the knowledge of the Son of God, to a mature man, to the measure of the stature which belongs to the fullness of Christ. [14] As a result, we are no longer to be children, tossed here and there by waves and carried about by every wind of doctrine, by the trickery of men, by craftiness in deceitful scheming; [15]but speaking the truth in love, we are to grow up in all aspects into Him who is the head, even Christ." We are not to be like children that have no stability. Spiritual maturity allows us to speak the truth to one another with love, so that we can all grow in maturity. That is what God wants of us.

The word of God is an integral part of our growth. Peter says, "Like newborn babies, long for the pure milk of the word, so that by it you may grow in respect to salvation" (1 Peter 2:2). We've all seen babies crave milk. That is how we must long for God's word, so that we might grow. But what if we do not crave it like we should? Then perhaps we have not focused our study on its proper purpose. We don't approach the word merely as a duty to be performed. We must realize that we cannot know Jesus without knowing His word, and the purpose of our study is to know Jesus.

As we seek spiritual growth, we should ask God for wisdom concerning our maturity. God desires for us to grow spiritually, and He has given us all we need to experience spiritual growth, but we must desire it and work towards it. We can ask God to increase our faith and knowledge of Him. Look at how the apostle Paul prayed for those in Colossae. "For this reason also, since the day we heard of it, we have not ceased to pray for you and to ask that you may be filled with the knowledge of His will in all spiritual wisdom and understanding, [10] so that you will walk in a manner worthy of the Lord, to please Him in all respects, bearing fruit in every good work and increasing in the knowledge of God" (Colossians 1:9-10). We can pray this prayer for ourselves and for others.

As the children's song says, "Read your bible and pray every day and grow, grow, grow."

For Further Study Read Colossians 1. What had Paul heard of the saints at Colossae? Look at the description of Christ in verses 13-23. Oh, the incomparable Christ! Investigate the terms "Lord" and "Savior".

BE HOLY

"But like the Holy One who called you, be holy yourselves also in all your behavior." 1 Peter 1:15

HOW JESUS IS HOLY:

Holiness is one of the fundamental descriptors of God. In Exodus 15:11, Moses asks, "Who is like you among the gods, O LORD? Who is like You, majestic in holiness, Awesome in praises, working wonders?" The answer to this rhetorical question is, of course, no one. The scriptures say that only God is holy. "For you alone are holy" (Revelation 15:4). Yet since God is holy, we know Jesus is holy, since Jesus has every characteristic of God.

But what does it mean that God is holy? One definition is "apartness." God is separate, apart from everything else. God is unique. He is separate from everything that is against His nature. He is only God, and He is the only God.

Two times in the scriptures (Isaiah 6:2-3 and Revelation 4:8), we read of the heavenly beings praising God with the expression "Holy, Holy, Holy." The repetition of "holy" is a forceful declaration. He is not barely holy, but holy through and through. He is infinitely unique, distinct, and sacred, and our worship should reflect our appreciation of His holiness.

Several times in scripture, Jesus is called holy, including:

- In his second recorded sermon, Peter said of the Jews, "But you disowned the Holy and Righteous One and asked for a murderer to be granted to you" (Acts 3:14).

76

- In Acts 4:27, the disciples prayed after the release of Peter and John, "For truly in this city there were gathered together against Your holy servant Jesus, whom You anointed, both Herod and Pontius Pilate, along with the Gentiles and the peoples of Israel." And, in that same prayer (verse 30), He was called "Your holy servant Jesus" again.

- The angel called Him the holy Child when he told Mary of his birth: "The angel answered and said to her, 'The Holy Spirit will come upon you, and the power of the Most High will overshadow you; and for that reason the holy Child shall be called the Son of God'" (Luke 1:35).

- An unclean spirit "believed and trembled" (James 2:19), saying, "What business do we have with each other, Jesus of Nazareth? Have You come to destroy us? I know who You are—the Holy One of God!" (Mark 1:24).

- In Acts 13:35, Paul, preaching to Jews in Pisidian Antioch, used Psalm 16:10 to convince them that Jesus was the promised Messiah. "You will not allow your holy one to undergo decay."

- In Hebrews 7:26, He was called a holy High Priest. "For it was fitting for us to have such a high priest, holy, innocent, undefiled, separated from sinners and exalted above the heavens."

Jesus remained perfectly holy because He never committed sin. 1 John 3:5 says, "You know that He appeared in order to take away sins; and in Him there is no sin." As a man, Jesus was fully subject to the capacity to sin, the temptation to sin, and the torment of resisting temptations. Praise the Lord that He refused temptation and remained holy and fit for our sacrifice.

HOW WE ARE TO BE HOLY:

We are told to be holy as God is holy. (1 Peter 1:15) But we are also told that only God is holy. So how do we resolve that seeming incongruity?

There are objects in scripture that are called holy. The Lord's temple is described as holy in Psalm 5:7 along with many other scriptures. What made that building holy? In Exodus 28:2 and others, Aaron's garments were described as holy garments. Again, what made the garments holy? In 1 Kings 8:4 and others, the tabernacle vessels were called holy. In Genesis 2:3, it says the seventh day was holy.

What made all these objects holy? They were to be used only in God's service. You would not gather in the temple for a school play, wear the holy garments to work on Monday, use the temple vessels to eat supper one night, or make Saturday just an ordinary day. God separated them all for *His* service, and this made them holy. God dictates what is holy.

In the same way that the objects are holy because God made them holy, we are holy because God has made us holy. We are separated and set apart for His service. As Peter wrote, we are a "holy nation" (1 Peter 2:9). The church, His people, belong to God and are dedicated to His service. Peter also said, "But like the Holy One who called you, be holy yourselves also in all your behavior." (1 Peter 1:15). The holy objects would be defiled if they were used for secular purposes. In the same way, we defile ourselves if we do not live a life devoted to God and separated from sin. We are set apart *to* God and *from* sin.

Holiness describes a unique relationship that God desires with his people. We desecrate that relationship by serving Satan or self. Also, holiness is not something we only "take time to be;" it is what we are. We are just as holy at work or at play as when we are at worship. We are holy if we are His faithful children.

For Further Study Holy or holiness is found almost 700 times in the King James Version of the Bible. God tells us to be holy as He is holy, so we need to know more about how He is holy, and how we can be holy. Do a word search and study each context.

HYMN

Holy, Holy, Holy Reginald Heber (1826) Public Domain

Holy, holy, holy
Lord God almighty
Early in the morning my song shall rise to Thee
Holy, holy, holy
Merciful and mighty
God in three persons, blessed Trinity

Holy, holy, holy
All the saints adore Thee
Casting down their golden crowns around the glassy sea
All the cherubim and seraphim are falling down before Thee
Which wert and art and evermore shalt be

Holy, holy, holy
Though the darkness hide Thee
Though the eyes of sinful man Thy glory may not see
Lord, only Thou art holy and there is none beside Thee
Perfect in power, in love and purity

Holy, holy, holy
Lord God almighty
All Thy works shall praise Thy name in earth and sky and sea
Holy, holy, holy
Merciful and mighty
God in three persons, blessed Trinity

HONEST AND TRUTHFUL

"Lying lips are an abomination to the Lord, But those who deal faithfully are His delight." Proverbs 12:22

HOW JESUS IS HONEST:

Honesty and truth is such an important topic in this time, called the "post-truth era." How sad, how tragic it is, if we cease to value honesty and truth. Just how important is truth? The word "truth" occurs 192 times in the NASB95. Truth saves (Psalm 69:13), it makes us free (John 8:32), and much more. Truth is defined by Webster's as "conformity to fact or reality; exact accordance with that which is, or has been; or shall be."

The modern idea of "your truth" and "my truth" is ridiculous. Truth is an absolute. When something is absolute, it means that it is not dependent upon anything else. Opinions are relative. They depend on biases and information and vary from person to person. I will have my opinion and you will have yours, but truth is just reality.

Consider the statement that God is real. That is either true or untrue. I may have an opinion about it, but that does not change the truth of it. Truth is also not dependent on whether people recognize it as truth. Truth is not established by consensus.

So is this just semantics, a much-to-do-about-nothing? No, because if we stop believing in absolute truth, society comes tumbling down.

Jesus is truth. In John 14:6, He said, "I am the way, and the truth, and the life; no one comes to the Father but through Me."

God abounds in truth. "Then the LORD passed by in front of him and proclaimed, 'The LORD, the LORD God, compassionate and gracious, slow to anger, and abounding in lovingkindness and truth'" (Exodus 34:6). Imagine what it would be like to serve a god that you could not trust to be truthful. Thank God for truth.

Jesus is the source of all truth. "And the Word became flesh, and dwelt among us, and we saw His glory, glory as of the only begotten from the Father, full of grace and truth" (John 1:14). In His great discourse on truth in John 8, Jesus said, "And you will know the truth, and the truth will make you free" (John 8:32).

Jesus spoke the truth. During His last days, the leaders sent men to trap Him. They said to Him, "Teacher, we know that You are truthful and defer to no one; for You are not partial to any, but teach the way of God in truth" (Mark 12:14). These men may have had ulterior motives for saying this, but it was certainly a true statement. Jesus was indeed truthful and would never tell a lie. He claimed to speak the truth in John 8:45: "But because I speak the truth, you do not believe Me."

When Jesus told Pilate that he had come into the world to testify of truth, Pilate said, "What is truth?" (John 18:37-38). Pilate seemed to scoff at the concept of truth, as if it were unattainable or unimportant. The irony is that this might be the most important question a person can ask, and Pilate is standing in front of the One who is the source of all truth. Yet he walks away without seeking truth from its only source. What a tragedy.

HOW WE MUST BE HONEST:

We must not, like Pilate, be scoffers at the whole concept of truth, but we must be genuine seekers of truth. We must...

Know the truth "And you will know the truth, and the truth will make you free" (John 8:32).

Obey the truth "But to those who are selfishly ambitious and do not obey the truth, but obey unrighteousness, wrath and indignation." (Romans 2:8-9).

Speak the truth "Therefore, laying aside falsehood, speak truth each one of you with his neighbor, for we are members of one another" (Ephesians 4:25).

Love in truth "Little children, let us not love with word or with tongue, but in deed and truth (1 John 3:18).

Other scriptures that show us the importance of truth:

Colossians 3:9-10 "Do not lie to one another, since you laid aside the old self with its evil practices, [10] and have put on the new self who is being renewed to a true knowledge according to the image of the One who created him."

Proverbs 12:22 "Lying lips are an abomination to the Lord, But those who deal faithfully are His delight."

I Peter 3:10 (quoted from Psalm 34:12) "The one who desires life, to love and see good days, Must keep his tongue from evil and his lips from speaking deceit."

1 Corinthians 13:6 Love "does not rejoice in unrighteousness, but rejoices in the truth."

Galatians 4:16 "So have I become your enemy by telling you the truth?" We should appreciate being told the truth, even if it hurts.

How much does God hate lying? Revelation 21:8 says, "But for the cowardly and unbelieving and abominable and murderers and immoral persons and sorcerers and idolaters and all liars, their part will be in the lake that burns with fire and brimstone, which is the second death."

What will we do if society continues to devalue truth and honesty? We, as the church, must continue to honor truth, and we must teach our children to tell the truth. Children tell lies for several reasons. Usually, they want to take control of a situation by changing the story to avoid getting into trouble. Age and development play a role, too. Young children may lie about something they wish were true, like telling people they're getting a pony when they are not. Teens may tell lies to hide things, primarily from their parents or teachers.

Children have to be taught that it is not right to lie, or they will become adults who lie. Some ways to do this include:

- Set an example of honesty – we tell the truth.

- Talk about honesty and make it a focus for the family.

- Praise honesty – reward truth telling.

- Tell them how happy honesty makes us and God.

- Practice calm, appropriate discipline if they fail.

For Further Study Consider the question, how much do I hate lying and love truth? Social media is a serious threat to our honesty. Christians will forward something that they really have no idea whether it is true or not. Is spreading a lie any better because it is on social media? Do a Bible search for "truth." Pray that our society will seek and value truth.

BE HUMBLE

"When pride comes, then comes dishonor,
But with the humble is wisdom." Proverbs 11:2

HOW JESUS IS HUMBLE:

Jesus' complete life showed a total and absolute absence of pride, arrogance, or vanity. From the moment of His birth, the Savior taught humility through example as the great Creator of all the heavens and the earth assented to be born in the humblest of circumstances. He put on mortality, not in a palace, but in a shelter for animals and was laid in a manger, a crib that was used for their feeding. His first visitors were humble shepherds (Luke 2:7-20). He was God—equal with the Father, sharing glory with Him, and having every privilege of God—and then He became a man and laid aside all those privileges. "He is the image of the invisible God" (Colossians 1:15). For God to become man is the essence of humility.

Philippians 2:5-8 says, "Have this attitude in yourselves, which was also in Christ Jesus, [6] who, although He existed in the form of God, did not regard equality with God a thing to be grasped, [7] but emptied Himself, taking the form of a bond-servant, and being made in the likeness of men. [8] Being found in appearance as a man, He humbled Himself by becoming obedient to the point of death, even death on a cross." It says Jesus "humbled himself" by *becoming obedient*. For further study on this, read the lesson *Obey like Jesus* (page #113).

Jesus had the power to come as the greatest earthly king ever to reign. He had the resources to live sumptuously in the most elegant surroundings. Yet in Matthew 8:20, He says that he did not even have a place to lay his head. We are told in 2 Corinthians 8:9 that he was willing to do this for our sakes. What a great expression of His love for us! "For you know the grace of our Lord Jesus Christ, that though He was rich, yet for your sake He became poor, so that you through His poverty might become rich." How grateful we are to God that Jesus was willing to do this for us.

The image of Jesus kneeling on the floor to wash his disciples' feet makes a profound impression on our hearts of our Lord's humility. The event is found in John 13. Notice verses 12-17. "So when He had washed their feet, and taken His garments and reclined at the table again, He said to them, 'Do you know what I have done to you? [13]You call Me Teacher and Lord; and you are right, for so I am. [14]If I then, the Lord and the Teacher, washed your feet, you also ought to wash one another's feet. [15]For I gave you an example that you also should do as I did to you. [16]Truly, truly, I say to you, a slave is not greater than his master, nor is one who is sent greater than the one who sent him. [17]If you know these things, you are blessed if you do them.'" Amen and amen.

Contrast what Jesus had with what He could have had and what He did with what He could have done. But He chose a lowly life. His life is the greatest example of humility ever lived.

HOW WE MUST BE HUMBLE:

Jesus was not telling us literally to wash His disciples' feet but giving us a principle of humility. Humility requires us to have a right view of ourselves in relation to others, and especially to God. It is an example of what the Spirit taught in Philippians 2:3: "Do nothing from selfishness or empty conceit, but with humility of mind regard one another as more important than yourselves."

Everything we will ever accomplish is a gift from God, and every accomplishment of our children or grandchildren is a gift from God. He made us and gave us every talent that we have. A truly grateful heart is a humble heart. Let us learn to thank God for every accomplishment, rather than secretly self-praise. The key to humility is "none of self and all of Thee."

Humility is the opposite of pride. Proverbs 16:18 tells us that, "Pride goes before destruction, And a haughty spirit before stumbling." Maybe we consider pride just a little sin, not as bad as others. But John lists it with the lust of the eyes and flesh in 1 John 2:16: "For all that is in the world, the lust of the flesh and the lust of the eyes and the boastful pride of life, is not from the Father, but is from the world." And "haughty eyes" is the very first thing on the list of things God hates (Proverbs 6:16-17a).

Here are other words of wisdom from the Proverbs that warn us away from pride and towards humility:

Proverbs 8:13 "The fear of the LORD is to hate evil; Pride and arrogance and the evil way And the perverted mouth, I hate."

Proverbs 11:2 "When pride comes, then comes dishonor, But with the humble is wisdom."

Proverbs 21:24 "'Proud,' 'Haughty,' 'Scoffer,' are his names, Who acts with insolent pride."

Proverbs 29:23 "A man's pride will bring him low, But a humble spirit will obtain honor."

In both letters to the Corinthians (1 Corinthians 1:31 and 2 Corinthians 10:17), to teach humility, Paul refers to Jeremiah 9:23-24 which reads, "Thus says the LORD, 'Let not a wise man boast of his wisdom, and let not the mighty man boast of his might, let not a rich man boast of his riches; [24] but let him who boasts boast of this, that he understands and knows Me, that I am the LORD who exercises lovingkindness, justice and righteousness on earth; for I delight in these things,' declares the LORD."

Now that is something to "boast" about: "I know God, and I have a relationship with Him." See the lesson on *Know like Jesus* (page #97). Our little piddling accomplishments, whatever they are—intelligence, riches, strength, or anything else—are nothing compared to the character of God and His Son and Holy Spirit.

Jesus told a story illustrating that the "religious" must not approach God in pride. He told of two men who entered the temple to pray (Luke 18:9–14). One was a Pharisee and one a tax collector. The first recited his pious deeds to God and thanked Him that he was not like other men, including the tax collector. The tax collector stood far off with downcast eyes and prayed humbly, "God, be merciful to me, the sinner!" (Luke 18:13). Jesus said the tax collector went home justified rather than the Pharisee and concluded the story: "Everyone who exalts himself will be humbled, but he who humbles himself will be exalted" (Luke 18:14). Let "God be merciful to me, the sinner" be our daily prayer, as we strive for humility.

For Further Study: Find more passages about being humble and meditate on them.

JUDGE

"And He will judge the world in righteousness;" Psalm 9:8

HOW JESUS JUDGES:

In Genesis 18:25, Abraham called God the Judge of all the earth. Psalm 9:7-8 says, "And He will judge the world in righteousness; He will execute judgment for the peoples with equity. Psalm 19:9 says, "The judgments of the Lord are true; they are righteous altogether." We thank God that He is righteous and loving towards us, and we can trust that His judgments are fair and equitable.

In John 5:22 and 27, Jesus reveals that the Father has given Him the power of divine judgment. "For not even the Father judges anyone, but He has given all judgment to the Son... ^{27}And He gave Him authority to execute judgment, because He is the Son of Man." This foretells Christ's eventual judgment of all mankind. "He [the Father] has fixed a day in which He will judge the world in righteousness through a Man whom He has appointed, having furnished proof to all men by raising Him from the dead" (Acts 17:31). "In the future there is laid up for me the crown of righteousness, which the Lord, the righteous Judge, will award to me on that day; and not only to me, but also to all who have loved His appearing" (2 Timothy 4:8).

All humanity will be judged by God the Son, Jesus Christ, based upon the deeds done in this life. The Bible says that each of us will be judged according to our works. Paul wrote, "Who will render to each person according to his deeds: ^{7} to those who by perseverance in doing good seek for glory and honor and immortality, eternal life; ^{8}but to those who are selfishly ambitious and do not obey the truth, but obey unrighteousness, wrath and indignation. There will be tribulation and distress for every soul of man who does evil, of the Jew first and also of the Greek, [10] but glory and honor and peace to everyone who does good, to the Jew first and also to the Greek. [11] For there is no partiality with God" (Romans 2:6-11).

Many think of the final judgement as a modern-day trial where we will stand before the judge and argue our case. No, those judgements are being made today, and at the end, they will be pronounced. At the final judgement, everyone will recognize Jesus as Lord. In two places (Romans 14:11 and Philippians 2:10), Paul refers to Isaiah 45:23: "To Me every knee will bow, every tongue will swear allegiance." We may refuse Him today, but everyone who has ever lived will be gathered at that judgment and will willingly recognize Christ as Lord.

God desires all men to be saved (2 Peter 3:9), but Jesus gave us grave warnings about punishment that is reserved for the unrighteous. "These will go away into eternal punishment, but the righteous into eternal life" (Matthew 25:46).

We must not question the judgment of the Lord but trust it. Consider loved ones gone before us. We should not worry about how they will be judged. They are in the hands of the loving, just, and righteous God. Our responsibility is to seek passionately to do His will so that we can stand before the Lord, clothed in Christ's righteousness, so that we might hear Him say, "Enter into the joy of your master" (Matthew 25:23).

HOW WE SHOULD JUDGE:

Jesus told us how to judge. In Matthew 7:1, one of the most often quoted, but least understood passages in the scriptures, Jesus says, "Do not judge so that you will not be judged." But He is condemning a particular *kind* of judging. He then tells us how to judge.

In the next verse, Jesus says, "For in the way you judge, you will be judged; and by your standard of measure, it will be measured to you." Teaching against judging in hypocrisy, He then uses a piercing analogy to warn of self-righteousness and hypocrisy. "Why do you look at the speck that is in your brother's eye, but do not notice the log that is in your own eye? [4] Or how can you say to your brother, 'Let me take the speck out of your eye,' and behold, the log is in your own eye? [5] You hypocrite, first take the log out of your own eye, and then you will see clearly to take the speck out of your brother's eye" (Matthew 7:3-5).

Imagine standing with a big two-by-four in your eye and not even recognizing it, but you see a tiny little speck in your brother's eye. How could you possibly help get that speck out of your brother's eye with a two-by-four in yours? But Jesus has a solution. He does not say just to leave the speck. He says to get the beam out of *your* eye and then help get the speck out of your brother's eye. In other words, straighten up your own life so that you can help your brother with his. See, it is really a lesson about hypocrisy, is it not?

When Jesus was defending Himself to the Jews for healing on the Sabbath, He said in John 7:24, "Do not judge according to appearance, but judge with righteous judgment." He pointed out that they circumcise on the Sabbath, so how could they criticize Him for making a man well on the Sabbath? They did not really care about defending the law; they were just seeking something with which to attack Jesus.

Romans 2:1 is also teaching against hypocrisy. "Therefore you have no excuse, every one of you who passes judgment, for in that which you judge another, you condemn yourself; for you who judge practice the same things." Paul had just finished describing the sins of the Gentiles whom God gave "over to a depraved mind, to do those things which are not proper" (Romans 1:28). But then he cautions the Jews to not think they could pass judgement on the Gentiles if they were also sinning. Verse 12 explains it further. "For all who have sinned without the Law will also perish without the Law, and all who have sinned under the Law will be judged by the Law."

It is impossible to fulfill our responsibilities as Christians if we fail to make judgments about right or wrong behavior in others, but that judgement must be for their good. Also, we are to use the same kind of fairness when we judge others that we want God to use with us. Here is one example from scriptures to show that to condemn sin in others is not violating Matthew 7:1.

Galatians 6:1: "Brethren, even if anyone is caught in any trespass, you who are spiritual, restore such a one in a spirit of gentleness; each one looking to yourself, so that you too will not be tempted." How could we obey this command without judging that someone is overtaken in sin? Yet, look how we are to do it: with gentleness and self-awareness of our own weakness.

So many times when we study this topic, we focus on the false teaching, (that Jesus said "don't judge"), and we should, because it is so prevalent. Yet we must not neglect the vital lesson that we *should* judge. The most unloving thing one can do is not approach fellow Christians about their sin. We must guard our hearts when we judge others, that we do it in the proper spirit. We also must be brave enough and caring enough to judge someone who is overtaken in sin and strive to help them.

For Further Study Find other passages that require that we judge others.

BE KIND

"The LORD is righteous in all His ways And kind in all His deeds."
Psalm 145:17

HOW JESUS IS KIND:

In Romans 2:4, we read "Or do you think lightly of the riches of His kindness and tolerance and patience, not knowing that the kindness of God leads you to repentance?" The Greek word *chrēstos* is translated kindness here, and Strong's says it means "mild and pleasant (as opposed to harsh, hard, sharp, bitter)." The Lord is not harsh in His treatment of us, but kind. As we meditate on this, it should cause us to be sorry for our transgressions and change.

The KJV translates this verse as "despisest thou the riches of his goodness..." This is a good time to talk about the meaning of this word "despise" in scripture. We generally use the English word "despise" as to detest or abhor, but when we see "despise" in scriptures (for example, Matthew 6:24; 18:10; Luke 16:13; 1 Corinthians 11:22; Hebrews 12:2; 2 Peter 2:10) it means to devalue or not esteem as highly as we should. So if we value God's kindness as highly as we should, it will lead us to repentance.

1 Peter 2:1-3 also says that tasting the "kindness of the Lord" will motivate us to do right. "Therefore, putting aside all malice and all deceit and hypocrisy and envy and all slander, ²like newborn babies, long for the pure milk of the word, so that by it you may grow in respect to salvation, ³if you have tasted the kindness of the Lord." Tasting the kindness of the Lord should cause us to treat others differently. Look at what he says to put away—malice, deceit, hypocrisy, envy, and slander. So we must conclude that if we practice such, we do not relish the Lord's kindness as we should.

92

Jesus is the kindness of God. Titus 3:4-5: "But when the kindness of God our Savior and His love for mankind appeared, [5] He saved us, not on the basis of deeds which we have done in righteousness, but according to His mercy, by the washing of regeneration and renewing by the Holy Spirit." "Appeared" may mean when Christ literally came to earth, or it may be a reference to the time a person accepts Christ. This is when God's goodness and lovingkindness "appear" in our lives.

Jesus said in Luke 6:35 that God is "kind to ungrateful and evil men." How is that? Remember that while we were yet sinners Christ died for us (Romans 5:8). Also, Jesus says that "He causes His sun to rise on the evil and the good and sends rain on the righteous and the unrighteous" (Matthew 5:45). God is kind to all mankind.

We see so many instances while Jesus was on earth of His kindness. He touched the untouchables. He let the little children come to Him. He ate meals with the rejects of society. He conversed with an "unacceptable" woman who'd had five husbands. He said to another woman, "I do not condemn you, either. Go and sin no more." He fed the hungry. He reached out to people who were sick, discouraged, beaten down, and humbled. No one was more kind to the common man than Jesus.

HOW WE ARE TO BE KIND:

Kindness is a universally approved moral principle. Who would ever say kindness is evil? And in the scriptures, it is tied to many other righteous behaviors. Ephesians 4:32 is probably the most familiar scripture that teaches kindness. "Be kind to one another, tender-hearted, forgiving each other, just as God in Christ also has forgiven you." Kindness is also fruit of the Spirit. "But the fruit of the Spirit is love, joy, peace, patience, kindness, goodness, faithfulness, [23] gentleness, self-control; against such things there is no law" (Galatians 5:22). As we live by the spirit of Christ, we will be kind.

We find kindness in the descriptors of love in 1 Corinthians 13. "Love is patient, love is kind and is not jealous; love does not brag and is not arrogant, [5] does not act unbecomingly; it does not seek its own, is not provoked, does not take into account a wrong suffered, [6] does not rejoice in unrighteousness, but rejoices with the truth; [7] bears all things, believes all things, hopes all things, endures all things."

Since we are holy and beloved of God, kindness is one of the characteristics that describes our hearts. "So, as those who have been chosen of God, holy and beloved, put on a heart of compassion, kindness, humility, gentleness and patience; [13] bearing with one another, and forgiving each other, whoever has a complaint against anyone; just as the Lord forgave you, so also should you" (Colossians 3:12-13).

Kindness requires:

- Desire—We have to want to be kind.

- Awareness—We must be cognizant of our behavior.

- Initiative—We have to *determine* to do it and then do it!

To make a habit of kindness, we must faithfully practice it. A Christian's kindness is not limited to a random act here or there when we happen to think of it. Kindness is a disposition of heart. We must be faithful every day to bear the good fruit of kindness in our thoughts, speech, and action. If we are mean spirited in our thoughts, it will be harder to be kind in our words and actions. Being kind should be our default mode, a habit of goodwill, and a heart of sweetness every day.

For Further Study: Make a list from scripture of kind deeds.

A hymn that we used to sing when we were children was *I Want to Be More Like Jesus* (J.M.Siillman). One verse and the refrain says:

HYMN

More Like Jesus

I want to be kind and gentle,
To those who are in distress;
To comfort the brokenhearted,
With sweet words of tenderness.

More and more like Jesus,
I would ever be;
More and more like Jesus,
My Savior who died for me.

Oh, yes, to be more and more like Jesus in our kindness!

KNOW

"So let us know, let us press on to know the LORD." Hosea 6:3

WHAT JESUS KNEW:

Let us read carefully John 10:14-15. Jesus said, "I am the good shepherd, and I know My own and My own know Me, [15] even as the Father knows Me and I know the Father; and I lay down My life for the sheep."

Jesus is our Good Shepherd and knows us. Jesus uses the word "know," not to just say that He has knowledge about us, but to express an intimate relationship of love. He is describing the relationship that He has with each of His sheep. And He elevates that relationship to even further heights when He compares it to His own intimate and cherished relationship with the Father. As God the Father loves Jesus, and Jesus loves the Father, Jesus loves His sheep, and His sheep love Him. Jesus is making a grand statement about our relationship with Him. It is like that of the Father and Son. How glorious that is!

Jesus knows us, everything about us. Psalm 44:21 says that He knows "the secrets of the heart." The entire Psalm 139 speaks of how thoroughly God knows us. "O Lord, You have searched me and known me. [2] You know when I sit down and when I rise up; You understand my thought from afar. [3] You scrutinize my path and my lying down And are intimately acquainted with all my ways. [4] Even before there is a word on my tongue, Behold, O Lord, You know it all. [5] You have enclosed me behind and before And laid Your hand upon me. [6] Such knowledge is too wonderful for me; It is too high; I cannot attain to it." It is a wonderful thing to David that God knows him so well. The key element of this knowing is that He loves us. He knows all our faults, but He still loves us. Does He love our faults? No, but He loves *us*. There is nowhere to hide from God, because He knows everything about us. That is why we can be completely honest with Him, because He knows us better than we know ourselves.

Notice also what Jesus knew from John 13:1. "Now before the Feast of the Passover, Jesus knowing that His hour had come that He would depart out of this world to the Father, having loved His own who were in the world, He loved them to the end." What great love! Even though Jesus knew the pain and suffering that He was about to endure, His love for humanity sustained to the end.

Jesus knew things man did not know:

- He knew men's hearts and thoughts (Matthew 9:4, 12:25; John 5:42).

- He knew the Father face to face (John 7:29).

- He knew when all things had been fulfilled (John 19:28).

When Jesus taught in the temple in John 7:15, it says, "The Jews then were astonished, saying, 'How has this man become learned, having never been educated?'" Remember that even at twelve years old, those in the temple were amazed at his understanding. Jesus had not been to one of their elite Jewish schools where He would have been taught the scriptures, but the Jews recognized His knowledge. His infinite knowledge is evidence for us to believe in Him. Thank God that He knows us and loves us.

HOW WE CAN KNOW GOD:

We can know God and the Lord Jesus Christ: not just know *about* them, but *know them*. When Jesus prayed for His disciples before His death, He prayed, "This is eternal life, that they may know You, the only true God, and Jesus Christ whom You have sent" (John 17:3).

The basics of knowing Jesus is recognizing Him as God. John says in John 1:10: "He was in the world, and the world was made through Him, and the world did not know Him." And John the Baptist said of Jesus, "I baptize in water, but among you stands One whom you do not know" (John 1:26).

All through his writings, the apostle John uses "know" to describe our relationship with God. In 1 John 2:3-6, he said, "By this we know that we have come to know Him if we keep His commandments. [4] The one who says, 'I have come to know Him,' and does not keep His commandments, is a liar, and the truth is not in him; [5] but whoever keeps His word, in him the love of God has truly been perfected. By this we know that we are in Him: [6] the one who says he abides in Him ought himself to walk in the same manner as He walked."

John says it here about as plainly as anyone can: our relationship with God is dependent on our obedience. If we do not keep His commandments, we do not know Him. People often get frustrated when the importance of obedience is stressed. But Jesus said that even *His* love of the Father was demonstrated by *His* obedience. "But so that the world may know that I love the Father, I do exactly as the Father commanded Me" (John 14:31). Just as Jesus' love for the Father is demonstrated by obedience, so is ours.

Paul was describing His relationship with God in 2 Timothy 1:12: "For this reason I also suffer these things, but I am not ashamed; for I know whom I have believed and I am convinced that He is able to guard what I have entrusted to Him until that day." It should be our constant goal to know God more. The prophet Hosea said, "So let us know, let us press on to know the LORD" (Hosea 6:3a).

The central theme of Paul's prayer in Ephesians 1 is that they would know God more deeply. "I do not cease making mention of you in my prayers; [17]that the God of our Lord Jesus Christ, the Father of glory, may give to you a spirit of wisdom and of revelation in the knowledge of Him. [18] *I pray that the eyes of your heart may be enlightened, so that you will know what is the hope of His calling, what are the riches of the glory of His inheritance in the saints*" (Ephesians 1:16-18). Do we pray to have a deeper relationship with God? When we study the scriptures, do we study with the goal of not just accumulating facts, but knowing Him better?

Not everyone will choose to know God. In 2 Thessalonians 1:8-9, the apostle Paul warned that Jesus would come "dealing out retribution to those who do not know God and to those who do not obey the gospel of our Lord Jesus. [9] These will pay the penalty of eternal destruction, away from the presence of the Lord and from the glory of His power." There is no reason for not knowing God. He wants us to know Him so much that He has revealed Himself to us. God is so good to know.

For Further Study Do a bible search for the word "know". Look how many times it is used in the scripture. Write down and study more scriptures that help us grow in knowing God.

LOVE

"Walk in love, just as Christ also loved you and
gave Himself up for us." Ephesians 5:2

HOW JESUS LOVES:

How marvelous is the love of God! In Romans 5:8 we read,
"But God demonstrates His own love toward us, in that while we
were yet sinners, Christ died for us." How incomprehensible it is
that the Infinite and Holy God loves us, even those who scorn His
goodness and reject His truth. Yet He loves us so deeply that for us
He would sacrifice His own Son (John 3:19; Romans 5:10). This
love is astounding!

Ephesians 3:19 describes the love of Christ which
"surpasses knowledge." Verses 17-19 read, "So that Christ may
dwell in your hearts through faith; and that you, being rooted and
grounded in love, [18] may be able to comprehend with all the saints
what is the breadth and length and height and depth, [19] and to know
the love of Christ which surpasses knowledge, that you may be
filled up to all the fullness of God." How could we doubt Jesus'
love when He suffered and died in our place? There is the evidence
of Jesus' great love for us. We praise and thank God for His love.

The apostle John said, "See what great love the Father has
lavished on us." (1 John 3:1a NIV). "See" the great love. God has
demonstrated His love so that we can see it. We do not have to
wonder if He loves us. Look at what He has done! God's love is
most clearly seen at the cross. How could we possibly see what
Jesus did at the cross and doubt His love?

The Spirit through John says, "We have come to know and
have believed the love which God has for us. God is love, and the

100

one who abides in love abides in God, and God abides in him" (1 John 4:16). Yet we must understand that God defines love, not us. We must never say something like, "God loves us too much to punish us." That is man's view of love, not God's. Hebrews 12:6 says, "For those whom the Lord loves He disciplines." God's love for man does not negate our responsibilities to Him.

Hymn

The Love of God, F. Lehman (1917) Public Domain

The love of God is greater far Than tongue or pen can ever tell.
It goes beyond the highest star And reaches to the lowest hell.
The guilty pair, bowed down with care, God gave His Son to win;
His erring child He reconciled And pardoned from his sin.

Refrain O love of God, how rich and pure!
How measureless and strong!
It shall forevermore endure— The saints' and angels' song.

When hoary time shall pass away
And earthly thrones and kingdoms fall;
When men who here refuse to pray,
On rocks and hills and mountains call;
God's love, so sure, shall still endure, All measureless and strong;
Redeeming grace to Adam's race— The saints' and angels' song.

Could we with ink the ocean fill,
And were the skies of parchment made;
Were every stalk on earth a quill, And every man a scribe by trade;
To write the love of God above Would drain the ocean dry;
Nor could the scroll contain the whole,
Though stretched from sky to sky.

HOW WE LOVE:

The Greek word *agape* in the New Testament describes the love of God for us, as well as the reciprocal love that we have for God. *Agape* love is the highest form of love, contrasted with *eros*, erotic love, and *philia*, brotherly love. *Agape* love is more than an emotion. It demonstrates itself through actions and commitment. God demonstrates His love for us by giving His Son, now how do we demonstrate our love for Him?

It is exciting to think of loving like Jesus! What a great joy to contemplate having that kind of heart. To begin to love like Jesus, we must first realize that it will be a life-long endeavor. We must want so much to love like Jesus that we will devote our lives to it. When we love like Him, we peel away layers of selfishness, resentment, anxiety, pettiness, and entitlement. We reflect on our shortcomings so that we can overcome them.

Jesus told us how to love and who to love. When asked what the greatest commandment in the Law was, He answered, "You shall love the Lord your God with all your heart, and with all your soul, and with all your mind.' [38] This is the great and foremost commandment. [39] The second is like it, 'You shall love your neighbor as yourself" (Matthew 22:36-40).

Love of God is not just a concept from the new law. God has always wanted man's love. In Deuteronomy 6:5, Moses gives the law that Jesus quoted. Then He told them again to love God in Deuteronomy 10:12, 11:1, 11:13, 11:22, 13:3, 19:9, 30:6, and 30:16. Joshua reminded them in Joshua 22:5 and 23:11 to heed the admonitions of Moses to love God. Psalm 31:23 says, "O love the LORD, all you His godly ones! And Daniel prayed, "Alas, O Lord, the great and awesome God, who keeps His covenant and lovingkindness for those who love Him and keep His commandments" (Daniel 9:4).

Jesus said the second greatest command is to love others, telling His disciples the world would know they were His by their love for one another (John 13:35). Loving like Jesus means we love others (1 John 3:16–17). Loving like Jesus means we will love our enemies (Matthew 5:44). Loving like Jesus means we care enough about the souls of others to tell them the gospel of Christ.

Consider the church in Corinth with all its problems, especially those related to spiritual gifts. Absence of true *agape* love was at the heart of nearly all their problems. In 1 Corinthians 13, Paul maps out love. First, he emphasizes that love must motivate all our actions. Even the loftiest of deeds gains a person nothing if not done in love (Verses 1–3). Then Paul deconstructs love into its components: patient, kind, not jealous; does not brag, not arrogant, does not act unbecomingly; does not seek its own, not provoked, does not take into account a wrong suffered, does not rejoice in unrighteousness, but rejoices with the truth, bears all things, believes all things, hopes all things, endures all things (Verses 4-7).

Putting love into practice is not always easy. Even those last phrases – love bears all things, believes all things, hopes all things, endures all things – can be tough. *Agape* love is limitless. It does not say, "I'll go this far and no farther; I'm not going to forgive you again; I'm not going to let you hurt me again; I cannot believe you again." That is not *agape* love. *Agape* love is Jesus' love. He will always forgive and give us a fresh start. Let us think of it this way: Jesus "bears all things, believes all things, hopes all things, endures all things." And that is our goal, as well.

We should pray to love as Jesus loves. With God's help, we will do the best we can. That is what God expects of us. It will be for us a life-long labor of love.

For Further Study Do a word search for love. Let a study of the scriptures teach us about how to love. Then put it into practice.

BE MEEK

"As the elect of God, holy and beloved, put on tender mercies, kindness, humility, meekness, longsuffering. " Colossians 3:12

HOW JESUS IS MEEK:

Imagine how kings in Jesus's day would enter a city. Surely there would be a grand procession with the king dressed in splendor surrounded by soldiers on great and powerful animals. In Matthew 21:5, Matthew references Zechariah 9:9 as he describes our King Jesus making His final entry into Jerusalem. "Say to the daughter of Zion, 'Behold your king is coming to you, humble, and mounted on a donkey, even on a colt, the foal of a donkey.'"

Vine's Dictionary says of the word *praus,* translated meek: "It must be clearly understood, therefore, that the meekness manifested by the Lord and commended to the believer is the fruit of power. The common assumption is that when a man is meek it is because he cannot help himself; but the Lord was 'meek' because he had the infinite resources of God at His command." Often we hear it described as "strength under control." It is also said that trained wild horses are an analogy for meekness — strong and powerful yet under control and willing to submit.

So the lesson for us—and for those who saw Jesus—is that He is the prophesied King who was to come. He chose this lowliness even though He had the "infinite resources of God at His command." He was not what the Jews had expected or wanted. He was not coming as a mighty conqueror to free them from their Roman captors. But he came in meekness, riding on a lowly donkey, just as prophesied.

Jesus was this kind of meek: power under control. He certainly was not timid or afraid of conflict. Jesus did not shrink back from confronting people when it was needed, but His true desire is for all to submit to the Lord. Jesus beckoned us to come to Him, saying, "I am meek and lowly in heart and ye shall find rest unto your souls" (Matthew 11:29 KJV). Other translations use "gentle and humble" instead, and indeed, we used this passage in the lesson on humility. But the word for meek here is the same word *praus*. As implied by Vines, the words are closely related, yet meek carries with it the idea of humble and gentle *by choice*. Does Jesus have the power to lay on us a heavy burden? Of course, He does, but He chooses not to. Thank God for the meekness of Jesus.

HYMN

Come Unto Me F. E. Belden, Public Domain

O heart bowed down with sorrow! O eyes that long for sight!
There's gladness in believing; In Jesus there is light.

Refrain: "Come unto me, all ye that labor,
and are heavy laden, and I will give you rest.
Take my yoke upon you, and learn of me;
for I am meek and lowly in heart:
and ye shall find rest unto your souls."

Divinest consolation Doth Christ the Healer give;
Art thou in condemnation? Repent, believe and live. [Refrain]

His peace is like a river, His love is like a song;
His yoke's a burden never; 'Tis easy all day long. [Refrain]

How We are to be Meek:

Where could we learn meekness today but by studying the scriptures? We certainly do not see it in the world's leaders—they are hardly humble and gentle by choice. Jesus chose meekness, and we must also.

Moses was another meek leader, i.e., the meekest person in all the earth (Numbers 12:3). Consider just one example. When the Lord saw the golden calf that the people had built, He said to Moses, "I have seen this people, and behold, they are an obstinate people. [10] Now then let Me alone, that My anger may burn against them and that I may destroy them; and I will make of you a great nation" (Exodus 32:9-10). Look what opportunity the Lord is offering Moses. *His* family could be one of the great nations of the earth. But instead, Moses entreated the Lord to reconsider and to remember His promise to Abraham, Isaac, and Jacob. The Lord did so. Thus began a cycle of rebellion by the people, anger from the Lord, and intercession by Moses. Moses could have intervened for himself, but no, it was always for the people. This was the meekness of Moses, and by it we are reminded of our Lord's intervention for all mankind.

Consider these admonitions of meekness for us, all from the KJV, and all using the noun form (*praotēs*) of *praus*. And as we read, let us remember "strength under control." Let us remember the trained wild horse: strong and powerful yet under control and willing to submit.

1 Corinthians 4:21 "What will ye? shall I come unto you with a rod, or in love, and in the spirit of meekness?"

Galatians 5:22-23 "But the fruit of the Spirit is love, joy, peace, longsuffering, gentleness, goodness, faith, Meekness, temperance: against such there is no law."

106

Galatians 6:1 "Brethren, if a man be overtaken in a fault, ye which are spiritual, restore such a one in the spirit of meekness; considering thyself, lest thou also be tempted."

Ephesians 4:2 "With all lowliness and meekness, with longsuffering, forbearing one another in love;"

Colossians 3:12 "Put on therefore, as the elect of God, holy and beloved, bowels of mercies, kindness, humbleness of mind, meekness, longsuffering;"

1 Timothy 6:11 "But thou, O man of God, flee these things; and follow after righteousness, godliness, faith, love, patience, meekness."

Titus 3:2 "To speak evil of no man, to be no brawlers, but gentle, shewing all meekness unto all men."

What a blessing it is to choose meekness. Jesus had the power to enter Jerusalem on a great white charger and to demand all mankind's obedience. Moses had the power to accept God's offer to father his own nation. Our opportunities will certainly not be that life shattering—perhaps just small, day-in-day-out choices—but let us, like the Lord and like Moses, determine to choose meekness. When we face confrontations, in our families, in the church, or at work, if we put others' needs and wishes before ours, we can feel blessed by our choice.

For Further Study Find other examples of people that demonstrated strength under control and gentleness by choice.

MOURN

"Godly sorrow brings repentance that leads to salvation."
2 Corinthians 7:10 NIV

HOW JESUS MOURNED:

Mourning is the state of being in deep grief. Isaiah, describing the mourning of the coming Messiah, says, "He was despised and forsaken of men, A man of sorrows and acquainted with grief; And like one from whom men hide their face He was despised, and we did not esteem Him.⁴ Surely our griefs He Himself bore, And our sorrows He carried; Yet we ourselves esteemed Him stricken, Smitten of God, and afflicted. ⁵ But He was pierced through for our transgressions, He was crushed for our iniquities; The chastening for our well-being fell upon Him, And by His scourging we are healed.⁶ All of us like sheep have gone astray, Each of us has turned to his own way; But the LORD has caused the iniquity of us all To fall on Him" (Isaiah 53:3-6).

Man, through our sins and our rejection, caused the mourning of the Lord. In the Garden of Gethsemane, we see him grieving, weeping over His coming death (Matthew 26:38). As prophesied, Jesus prayed a psalm of lament on the cross, crying out, "My God, my God, why have you forsaken me?" (Matthew 27:46, Psalm 22:1). Because of His great love, our Lord and Savior was willing to undergo this great mourning.

Twice Luke records how Jesus mourned over the sins of the city of Jerusalem. In Luke 13:34, He says, "O Jerusalem, Jerusalem, the city that kills the prophets and stones those sent to her! How often I wanted to gather your children together, just as a hen gathers her brood under her wings, and you would not have it!" Throughout Israel's long history, the people had rejected God's prophets and spurned their message of repentance, pouring out rejection and scorn. And now the Promised One, Israel's Messiah and King, had come, and they likewise rejected Him.

This image of the mother hen protecting its young is used in the Old Testament for God's protection of his people (Deuteronomy 32:10-12, Psalm 17:8; 91:4; Isaiah 31:5). One can hear the pain in Jesus' voice. Surely, Jesus feels not self-pity, but sorrow for them in their lost condition. Here we see the depth of Jesus' feelings for lost people and for His beloved city that would soon be destroyed. Would not revenge have been a natural reaction to their rejection? But Jesus took no pleasure in denouncing the religious establishment or in prophesying the city's coming destruction. He had come to save, but they would not let Him.

The second event is recorded in Luke 19:41 as Jesus made the triumphal entry. As He approached Jerusalem, He saw the city and wept over it as He described its horrible coming destruction. Vine's says that this word translated "wept" means "any loud expression of grief." Jesus did not relish the destruction that Jerusalem was about to endure, rather He wept over it in the view of the surrounding multitude, lifting up his voice and lamenting aloud the calamities which He foresaw coming upon it.

Our sin and rejection cause great grief to the Lord, but He "desires all men to be saved and to come to the knowledge of the truth" (1 Timothy 2:4). It gives great joy for God to save men. "I tell you that in the same way, there will be more joy in heaven over one sinner who repents than over ninety-nine righteous persons who need no repentance" (Luke 19:7).

OUR MOURNING:

Just like Jesus, Christians are to have tender, compassionate hearts that grieve at times, and sin is the greatest reason for grief. We must not take sin lightly. When we sin, if we merely shrug our shoulders with a flippant "Sorry about that," we do not understand the enormity of sin.

Our sin cost Jesus His life. It severs our relationship with God. Left to germinate, the seeds of sin will become our heart's delight. Jesus told the Jews that whoever commits sin is the slave of sin (John 8:34). We do not want sin for a master. As the familiar saying goes, sin will take us farther than we want to go, keep us longer than we want to stay, and cost us more than we want to pay. Sin is a brutal taskmaster. Sin's pleasures are small and passing (Hebrews 11:24-26), while its griefs are brutal and can last a lifetime.

We must never feel above sin. In 1 Corinthians 10:12, Paul warns that we had better be careful if we think we cannot sin, "lest we fall." What do we do when we find ourselves enslaved by sin?

We must first mourn over it. 2 Corinthians 7:10 says, "Godly sorrow brings repentance that leads to salvation" (NIV). When the Prodigal Son woke up in the pigpen, he realized, "Father, I have sinned against heaven and before you, and I am no longer worthy to be called your son" (Luke 15:19). Think of Peter after he had denied the Lord at His trial and crucifixion. The Scriptures say that the Lord turned and looked at Peter, and "he went out and wept bitterly" (Luke 22:62). That is mourning. How devastating that must have been for Peter.

Godly sorrow leads to repentance when it produces the resolve to sin no longer. God will replace our sorrow with joy through repentance. In Psalm 51:10-12, David said, "Create in me a clean heart, O God, and renew a steadfast spirit within me.[11] Do not cast me from Your presence And do not take Your Holy Spirit from me.[12] Restore to me the joy of Your salvation and sustain me with a willing spirit."

God's ultimate purpose is not that we mourn but that we reject sin. Remember what Jesus told the woman brought to Him who had been caught in adultery: "From now on sin no more" (John 8:11). This is what Jesus wants for us: the joy of salvation. Remembrances of the pain of sin will help us to avoid sin in the future. When we are tempted to sin, we should say to ourselves, "No, I remember the pain of sin. I do not want that again." Read the lesson on Comfort (page #17).

For Further Study Find other scriptures that show the gravity of sin or what our attitude should be toward it? Read Revelation 21:4. God will wipe away every tear from our eyes. What a beautiful image.

HYMN

I Bring My Sins to Thee F. Havergal (1870) Public Domain

I bring my sins to Thee,
The sins I cannot count,
That all may cleansed be
In Thy once opened Fount;
I bring them, Savior, all to Thee;
The burden is too great for me, [repeat]

I bring my grief to Thee,
The grief I cannot tell;
No words shall needed be,
Thou knowest all so well;
I bring the sorrow laid on me,
O suffering Savior, all to Thee. [repeat]

BE OBEDIENT

"But so that the world may know that I love the Father, I do exactly as the Father commanded Me." John 14:31

HOW JESUS OBEYED:

Jesus lived a life of perfect obedience to His Father while on earth--not to be discounted as a simple feat. Jesus knows through experience what it means to be tempted to sin. Hebrews 5:8-9: "Although He was a Son, He learned obedience from the things which He suffered. [9] And having been made perfect, He became to all those who obey Him the source of eternal salvation."

Jesus sought to do the will of the Father. In John 5:30 Jesus says, "I can do nothing on My own initiative. As I hear, I judge; and My judgment is just, because I do not seek My own will, but the will of Him who sent Me." In Hebrews 10:7, He says He had come to do the will of God, fulfilling a prophecy found in Psalm 40:7–8.

So how was Jesus able to accomplish this perfect obedience? In the garden, as Jesus agonized with the thoughts of what He was soon to suffer, He prayed, "Father, if You are willing, remove this cup from Me; yet not My will, but Yours be done." Jesus fought temptation with prayer. To His apostles, He said, "Pray that you may not enter into temptation" (Luke 22:40). And then again when He found them sleeping: "Get up and pray that you may not enter into temptation" (Luke 22:40-46).

The Lord gave another reason for His obedience in John 14:31: "But so that the world may know that I love the Father, I do exactly as the Father commanded Me." He obeyed to show the world His love for the Father. Jesus can claim to love the Father because He obeys Him.

What a great example Jesus left us. His obedience came from a heart of love.

HYMN

Have Thine Own Way Lord A. Pollard (1906) Public Domain

Have thine own way, Lord! Have thine own way!
Thou art the potter, I am the clay.
Mold me and make me after thy will,
while I am waiting, yielded and still.

Have thine own way, Lord! Have thine own way!
Search me and try me, Savior today!
Wash me just now, Lord, wash me just now,
as in thy presence humbly I bow.

Have thine own way, Lord! Have thine own way!
Wounded and weary, help me I pray!
Power, all power, surely is thine!
Touch me and heal me, Savior divine!

Have thine own way, Lord! Have thine own way!
Hold o'er my being absolute sway.
Fill with thy Spirit till all shall see
Christ only, always, living in me!

How We Are Obedient:

Jesus put it very clearly: "If you love Me, you will keep My commandments" (John 14:15). If we do not obey, the logical conclusion is that we do not love Jesus. When we fail to obey, we have to admit that our love has failed.

Joseph gives us a wonderful example of obedience when Potiphar's wife tried to make him sin sexually. In Genesis 39:9b, Joseph asked her, "How could I do this great evil and sin against God?" Have we ever asked ourselves that question when we are tempted to sin? Do we realize the gravity of disobedience, because, as Jesus said, "If you love me, you will keep my commandments"?

In 1 John 5:3, not only did John stress that keeping God's commandments shows our love for God, he said that His commands are not "burdensome." God's will is good for us. It is not a burden. If we love Jesus, and if we love God, we will strive to obey.

It is impossible to name one command that is bad for us. God's way is the best way for us to live, and we must trust that. When God told Abram to go from his country, his people, and his father's household to the land He would show him, Abram did what God told him even if he had no idea where God was taking him (Genesis 12:1). Why did he do that? Because he trusted God.

How can we avoid sin? Jesus told his disciples, "Pray that you may not enter into temptation." How fervently Jesus prayed in the garden. Do we fervently pray when we are tempted to sin?

We are not perfect in our love, and we are not perfect in our obedience. But when we disobey, our hearts must grieve that we have failed in our love. Nothing can help us in this more than reading Psalm 51. How it grieved David that he had failed the Lord, but he knew that God yearned for him to turn back to Him.

We must turn away from sin and back to God. We must pray, "Create in me a clean heart, O God, And renew a steadfast spirit within me" (Psalm 51:10). God will restore us. Read Luke 15 and see the joy of the Father to have his rebellious son return.

We have probably sung the old hymn "Trust and Obey" hundreds of times. But do we really consider its words? Trust and obey, for there's no other way To be happy in Jesus, but to trust and obey."

For Further Study: Let us examine ourselves to see where we need to grow in our obedience. Let us pray to God for forgiveness and strength and joy in every step towards full obedience and love.

HYMN

Trust and Obey J. Sammis (1887) Public Domain

When we walk with the Lord in the light of His Word,
What a glory He sheds on our way!
While we do His good will, He abides with us still,
And with all who will trust and obey.

Refrain: Trust and obey, for there's no other way
To be happy in Jesus, but to trust and obey.

Then in fellowship sweet we will sit at His feet.
Or we'll walk by His side in the way.
What He says we will do, where He sends we will go;
Never fear, only trust and obey. Refrain

BE ONE

"Let the peace of Christ rule in your hearts, to which indeed you were called in one body; and be thankful." Colossians 3:15

HOW JESUS IS ONE:

There is one God. In Malachi 2:10, God's word says, "Do we not all have one father? Has not one God created us?" And Paul wrote in three places in the New Testament explicitly that there is "one God" (1 Corinthians 8:6; Ephesians 4:6; 1 Timothy 2:5). In His prayer, Jesus stated that God is the one true God. "This is eternal life, that they may know You, the only true God, and Jesus Christ whom You have sent" (John 17:3).

In today's world the belief in one God is quite common, but consider that throughout history, multiple gods were worshipped across most of the world. Even King Solomon fell into idolatry. "For Solomon went after Ashtoreth the goddess of the Sidonians and after Milcom the detestable idol of the Ammonites" (1 Kings 11:5). Idolatry was still prevalent in New Testament times, and some Christians were former idolaters (Galatians 4:8). So when the apostle Paul said, "Therefore, my beloved, flee from idolatry" (1 Cor. 10:14), he was speaking literally.

In John 10:30, Jesus declares something about oneness when He says, "I and the Father are one." Vine's says that this means union and accord. In other words, Jesus is saying that there is perfect agreement between Him and the Father.

Shortly before His ascension, Jesus said to the twelve, "Go therefore and make disciples of all the nations, baptizing them in

116

the name of the Father and the Son and the Holy Spirit" (Matthew 28:19), naming the three Persons in the Godhead. God is not made up of three gods, but He is a unity of three persons. A similar usage about man is found in Ezra 3:1, "Now when the seventh month came, and the sons of Israel were in the cities, the people gathered together as one man to Jerusalem." This oneness denotes unity. They were of one mind and acted as one. (Also read Judges 20:1 and Nehemiah 8:1 for similar usage.)

God's unity provides agreement. There is never even the slightest disagreement among the Father, Son, and Holy Spirit. When Jesus spoke, He spoke as the Father spoke. When the Holy Spirit came alongside to inspire the Scriptures (2 Peter 1:21), He spoke as the Father and Son spoke. We can trust that. In all things they speak and act as One.

As one of His last acts before His arrest, Jesus proclaimed His unity with the Father and asked for unity for His followers. John 17:10-11 says, "and all things that are Mine are Yours, and Yours are Mine; and I have been glorified in them. [11] I am no longer in the world; and yet they themselves are in the world, and I come to You. Holy Father, keep them in Your name, the name which You have given Me, that they may be one even as We are."

Again, in verses 20-21, He prays for ones that believe through the apostles' word. That would include us, so Jesus is praying here for us, that we might be one. "I do not ask on behalf of these alone, but for those also who believe in Me through their word; [21] that they may all be one; even as You, Father, are in Me and I in You, that they also may be in Us, so that the world may believe that You sent Me."

How We Can Be One:

We just read how the Lord prayed for us to be one as He and the Father are one. If Jesus prayed for our unity on the last day before his crucifixion, don't you think it is important?

Paul wrote in Ephesians 4:1-6, "Therefore I, the prisoner of the Lord, implore you to walk in a manner worthy of the calling with which you have been called, [2] with all humility and gentleness, with patience, showing tolerance for one another in love, [3] being diligent to preserve the unity of the Spirit in the bond of peace. [4] There is one body and one Spirit, just as also you were called in one hope of your calling; [5] one Lord, one faith, one baptism, [6] one God and Father of all who is over all and through all and in all."

Here Paul gives the source of our unity— "the unity of the Spirit." In other words, the unity we pursue is unity based on truth. Unity gains virtue only from its source. Indeed, Herod and Pilate were united in their common rejection of Jesus (Luke 23:12), but obviously that unity was not pleasing to God. True unity that pleases the Lord is only possible with a shared belief in truth.

Romans 15:5-6: "Now may the God who gives perseverance and encouragement grant you to be of the same mind with one another according to Christ Jesus, [6] so that with one accord you may with one voice glorify the God and Father of our Lord Jesus Christ."

Having heard that there were quarrels among them, Paul wrote to the church at Corinth in 1 Corinthians 1:10: "Now I exhort you, brethren, by the name of our Lord Jesus Christ, that you all agree and that there be no divisions among you, but that you be made complete in the same mind and in the same judgment." We are to be one like the Father and Son are one. We cannot even imagine them quarreling. Wouldn't it be wonderful if we could say,

118

"I cannot even imagine Christians quarreling"? Cynthia's daddy used to say if you tied two cats together by the tails and throw them over a clothesline, you would have union, but not unity.

The hymn, "How Sweet, How Heavenly" (Joseph Swain) captures our oneness in such beautiful language:

How sweet, how heavenly is the sight,
When those that love the Lord
In one another's peace delight, And so fulfill His Word.

Colossians 3:15: "Let the peace of Christ rule in your hearts, to which indeed you were called in one body; and be thankful." Nothing is more painful than being with a church group that is not getting along. So let us be thankful for unity.

For Further Study: How important is unity to us? Are we willing to yield our will to others when truth is not at stake? It takes selflessness that we must work to cultivate.

HYMN

Bless Be the Tie That Binds *J.* Fawcett (1782) Public Domain

Blessed be the tie that binds Our hearts in Christian love;
The fellowship of kindred minds Is like to that above.

We share each other's woes, Our mutual burdens bear;
And often for each other flows The sympathizing tear.

When we asunder part, It gives us inward pain;
But we shall still be joined in heart, And hope to meet again.

PATIENT

"Love is patient." 1 Corinthians 13:4a

HOW JESUS IS PATIENT:

The scriptures use "patience" in two ways: 1) longsuffering towards others and 2) perseverant and enduring. We determine from the context in which sense it is being used.

In 2 Peter 3, Peter described the mocking of unbelievers concerning the second coming of Christ (verses 3-4). Then, in verse 8-9, he writes, "But do not let this one fact escape your notice, beloved, that with the Lord one day is like a thousand years, and a thousand years like one day. The Lord is not slow about His promise, as some count slowness, but is patient toward you, not wishing for any to perish but for all to come to repentance." Since Christ had not returned yet, the skeptics denied both the Christ and the second coming. Rather, Peter says that the fact that Christ has not come yet is a display of God's patience. What a great comfort it is that the Lord perseveres with us so that we might come to repentance.

Patience is depicted as an element of the Lord's character in Psalm 145:8 as He is "slow to anger.": "The Lord is gracious and merciful; Slow to anger and great in lovingkindness." This sentiment is repeated many times in the Old Testament, with the exact phrase "slow to anger" occurring nine times (NASB95) describing the Lord. Are we not grateful for this attribute of God— His patience with us?

It is what Jonah recognized when he refused to go to preach to Nineveh. Was he complaining later that God had spared

Nineveh when he prayed, "Please Lord, was not this what I said while I was still in my own country? Therefore in order to forestall this I fled to Tarshish, for I knew that You are a gracious and compassionate God, slow to anger and abundant in lovingkindness, and one who relents concerning calamity" (Jonah 4:2)?

Consider the many times through Jewish history that God showed this patience—for instance, the cyclic period of the judges. The people would rebel, then God would bring judgment against them through foreign oppression. This horrible oppression would cause them to turn back to God, and He would raise up a deliverer to bring peace to the land. The people would be faithful for a while, but then fall back into sin, starting the cycle all over again. God sent twelve different deliverers (judges) to bring the people back to Him. What great patience. And we very often have trouble forgiving a second time!

Jesus was longsuffering with His disciples despite their lack of faith and their slowness to recognize and understand His divine mission. In their times of little faith, Jesus did not berate them or lose His temper. Yes, he would admonish them at times, but in a spirit of gentleness and compassion. Perhaps His strongest rebuke was when Peter denied prophecy of what was to happen to Him. "But turning around and seeing His disciples, He rebuked Peter and said, 'Get behind Me, Satan; for you are not setting your mind on God's interests, but man's'" (Mark 8:33). He was patient with the multitudes as they pressed about Him, with the woman taken in sin, with those who sought His healing power, and with little children. In patience, as in all things, He is our perfect example.

HOW WE ARE PATIENT:

Patience is a challenge for many of us. We want what we want when we want it, meaning now! But patience is something that we must cultivate. When describing love, Paul wrote, "Love is patient." (1 Corinthians 13:4a). Patience is easy to say, sometimes very hard to do, but essential. And what joy it gives to be like Jesus.

Patience in scriptures sometimes means perseverance and endurance. In James 5:7, James wrote, "Therefore be patient, brethren, until the coming of the Lord. The farmer waits for the precious produce of the soil, being patient about it, until it gets the early and late rains. [8] You too be patient; strengthen your hearts, for the coming of the Lord is near." In the KJV, Hebrews 10:36, says, "For ye have need of patience, that, after ye have done the will of God, ye might receive the promise."

Today, when someone patiently endures great hardships, we say they have "the patience of Job." James refers to Job in James 5:11 as he exhorts the brethren to endure. "You have heard of the endurance of Job and have seen the outcome of the Lord's dealings, that the Lord is full of compassion and is merciful." James is saying the outcome was worth what Job endured. And so it is for us. "Just one glimpse of Him in glory will the toils of life repay" ("When We All Get to Heaven," Eliza Hewitt).

Patience also means kind and gentle treatment of others. Not only is God "slow to anger," but four times in Proverbs we are also told to be slow to anger:

Proverbs 14:29 He who is slow to anger has great understanding, But he who is quick-tempered exalts folly.

Proverbs 15:18 A hot-tempered man stirs up strife, But the slow to anger calms a dispute.

Proverbs 16:32 He who is slow to anger is better than the mighty, And he who rules his spirit, than he who captures a city.

Proverbs 19:11 A man's discretion makes him slow to anger, And it is his glory to overlook a transgression.

Wise words indeed! We should not be easily annoyed or irritated, and we surely should not lose our temper. How do we accomplish this? We work at it. We pray for it. We work at becoming more like Jesus.

We all face situations that try our patience; we talk of "losing" our patience. What about something as trivial as waiting in line? Do we have so little patience that we get irritated with others when we have to wait, or do we accept it with grace? Do we treat those around us with kindness and gentleness so that they can see Christ living in us?

What about co-workers or perhaps members of our families when they make mistakes? Are we gentle with our corrections, or do we lose our patience? If we lose patience, what then? What we must *not* do is shrug our shoulders with an, "oh well, that's just me." We must not take it lightly. A sincere apology is fitting. "I am sorry I lost my patience with you, and I pray to God to help me to never treat you that way again." It is of paramount importance to show this to our children. They can certainly try our patience but let them see our humility and regret if we fail.

Patience requires strength of character. It requires restraint, calm and composure, all traits that must be cultivated. Babies are not very patient but demand that their needs be met immediately! That makes patience a life-long effort for all of us.

For Further Study: Can you find other examples in the scriptures of patience? Is it the perseverant or longsuffering meaning? Reflect on your own challenges with patience and pray for it.

MAKE PEACE

"And the peace of God, which surpasses all comprehension, will guard your hearts and your minds in Christ Jesus." Phil. 4:7

HOW JESUS IS A PEACEMAKER:

Peace is a beautiful concept, is it not? Defined as tranquility, absence of conflict, or freedom from disturbance, peace can refer to a number of different types of relationships—peace among nations, among individuals, even inner peace—but our most pressing need is peace with God. Sin robs us of that peace we have with God. Because we all sin (Romans 3:23), we are all sinners at war with God until we lay down our arms and submit to Him as our king.

Jesus is the supreme peacemaker. When Isaiah prophesied in Isaiah 9:6 of the child to come he said He was to be called, "Wonderful Counselor, Mighty God, Eternal Father, Prince of Peace." We sometimes think of a prince as a kind of soft Disney character, but Prince here means "ruler" or "captain". He would be the ruler of peace, its commander. When the angel announced Jesus' birth, a multitude of the heavenly host appeared saying, "Glory to God in the highest, And on earth peace among men with whom He is pleased" (Luke 2:14). It was heaven's proclamation that this was the Ruler of peace come to bring peace to mankind.

The role of the Prince of Peace helps to explain why Jesus disappointed His countrymen when He came. They wanted a monarch who would establish peace by obliterating their foes and reestablishing the glory Israel had known in the golden days of David and Solomon. They wanted Rome and any other oppressors to be crushed. Then they would have peace. But Jesus did not lift a finger against Rome, nor did He make any international peace treaties. The Jews did not want this kind of peaceful prince.

The peace that the Prince of Peace brought is described in Romans 5:1: "Therefore, having been justified by faith, we have peace with God through our Lord Jesus Christ." Verse 10 says, "For if while we were enemies we were reconciled to God through the death of His Son, much more, having been reconciled, we shall be saved by His life." The peace of Jesus is more than a ceasefire. It changes us from enemies of God into children of God. John said in John 1:11-12: "He came to His own, and those who were His own did not receive Him. [12] But as many as received Him, to them He gave the right to become children of God, even to those who believe in His name."

But what about where Jesus said he came *not* to bring peace, but a sword? (Matthew 10:34-37). Jesus was speaking to His apostles, readying them to go out to preach, teaching them about the true meaning of discipleship. Jesus' message, this "sword" they took out to the people, would divide the world into those who believe and those who do not. Jesus said it would even divide families, forcing many to make a difficult choice. Choosing Jesus gives the peace with God that He brings, but it may divide us from those we love.

Thank God for this infinite peace that we have through Jesus' blood on the cross. What a treasure is ours in Isaiah's predicted Messiah. He is our Prince of Peace. May we give Him our full devotion, as we ponder the great God that He is!

HOW WE MAKE PEACE:

In the Beatitudes, Jesus said, "Blessed are the peacemakers, for they shall be called sons of God." We have already talked of how Jesus came to give peace. When we accept Jesus, the Prince of peace, we become peacemakers. We have made peace with God and are called His children.

Consider this description of what God's peace will do for us. "Be anxious for nothing, but in everything by prayer and supplication with thanksgiving let your requests be made known to God. And the peace of God, which surpasses all comprehension, will guard your hearts and your minds in Christ Jesus" (Philippians 4:6-7). Look at what God's peace will do: "guard your hearts and your minds in Christ Jesus." God's peace produces a heart and mind free from worries. When we take our worries in prayer to the Father *with thanksgiving,* He grants an inner peace based on our unwavering confidence in God.

In a context of how to treat one another, Paul says, "Put on a heart of compassion, kindness, humility, gentleness and patience; [13] bearing with one another, and forgiving each other, whoever has a complaint against anyone; just as the Lord forgave you, so also should you. [14] Beyond all these things put on love, which is the perfect bond of unity." Then he adds, "Let the peace of Christ rule in your hearts, to which indeed you were called in one body; and be thankful" (Colossians 3:13-15). In Christ, we are peacemakers one with another.

These days we talk about creating "drama" meaning causing trouble. You see folks who just cannot seem to be happy unless they are stirred up about something. The news media literally thrives on stirring us to anger, and politics can be so divisive that families cannot discuss it without warring amongst themselves. This ought not to be. Let us be peacemakers, not troublemakers. And we certainly must be careful not to intervene with others' quarrels uninvited. Solomon warns in Proverbs 26:17, "Like one who takes a dog by the ears Is he who passes by and meddles with strife not belonging to him."

For Further Study: You may be surprised how many times the word peace is found in the scriptures. Do a word search for "peace" and study the verses that you find.

HYMN

Sweet Peace, the Gift of God's Love P. Bilhorn (1887) Public Domain

There comes to my heart one sweet strain,
A glad and a joyous refrain; I sing it again and again,
Sweet peace, the gift of God's love.

Refrain: Peace, peace, sweet peace! Wonderful gift from above!
Oh, wonderful, wonderful peace!
Sweet peace, the gift of God's love!

Through Christ on the cross peace was made,
My debt by His death was all paid;
No other foundation is laid
For peace, the gift of God's love. (Refrain)

When Jesus as Lord I had crowned,
My heart with this peace did abound;
In Him the rich blessing I found,
Sweet peace, the gift of God's love. (Refrain)

In Jesus for peace I abide, And as I keep close to His side,
There's nothing but peace doth betide,
Sweet peace, the gift of God's love. (Refrain)

PLEASE GOD

"Walk in a manner worthy of the Lord, to please Him in all respects." Colossians 1:10

HOW JESUS PLEASED GOD:

God left no doubt that He was pleased with His Son. Twice during His earthly ministry, the Father decreed it from heaven: "After being baptized, Jesus came up immediately from the water; and behold, the heavens were opened, and he saw the Spirit of God descending as a dove and lighting on Him, [17] and behold, a voice out of the heavens said, 'This is My beloved Son, in whom I am well-pleased'" (Matthew 3:16-17). Then, again in Matthew 17:5-7, at the transfiguration of Jesus: "While he was still speaking, a bright cloud overshadowed them, and behold, a voice out of the cloud said, 'This is My beloved Son, with whom I am well-pleased; listen to Him!'"

You hear tenderness and love in the Father's words. He calls Jesus "beloved" and says that He is well pleased with Him. God is love (1 John 4:16). Love is prevalent in who He is and what He does. What Jesus is doing pleases the Father, because He wants to save mankind, yet because of His love for the Son, it must torture Him to witness what man does to Him.

These words firmly confirmed to all who heard them, and now to all who read them, that Jesus is the Messiah sent by God. Look at what an impact they had on the apostle Peter. He wrote, "For we did not follow cleverly devised tales when we made known to you the power and coming of our Lord Jesus Christ, but we were eyewitnesses of His majesty. [17] For when He received honor and glory from God the Father, such an utterance as this was made to Him by the Majestic Glory, 'This is My beloved Son with whom I

128

am well-pleased'— [18] and we ourselves heard this utterance made from heaven when we were with Him on the holy mountain" (2 Peter 1:16-18). Consider being there and witnessing this great event.

Jesus said He always does the things that please the Father in John 8:28-29: "When you lift up the Son of Man, then you will know that I am He, and I do nothing on My own initiative, but I speak these things as the Father taught Me. [29] And He who sent Me is with Me; He has not left Me alone, for I always do the things that are pleasing to Him."

In one of Isaiah's great Messianic prophecies, he declared, "Behold, My Servant, whom I uphold; My chosen one in whom My soul delights. I have put My Spirit upon Him; He will bring forth justice to the nations" (Isaiah 42:1). Matthew references and applies it to Jesus when he wrote, "This was to fulfill what was spoken through Isaiah the prophet: 'Behold, My Servant whom I have chosen; My Beloved in whom My soul is well-pleased; I will put My Spirit upon Him'" (Matthew 12:18).

In Colossians 1:19, Paul says, "For it was the Father's good pleasure for all the fullness to dwell in Him," emphasizing the incarnation of Jesus, coming to us in human form, while remaining fully God. This verse closely reflects John 1:14: "And the Word became flesh and dwelt among us." Jesus "set up His tent" among us, taking on the same body as a mortal human being, identifying with our human weaknesses and limitations. Jesus willingly became human to die as a perfect sacrifice for the sins of man. And that pleased the Father greatly.

HOW WE CAN PLEASE GOD:

The apostle Paul wrote in Ephesians 5:8-10: "For you were formerly darkness, but now you are Light in the Lord; walk as children of Light (for the fruit of the Light consists in all goodness and righteousness and truth), trying to learn what is pleasing to the Lord."

As the Hebrew writer closes the letter, he tells us what pleases God. "Now the God of peace, who brought up from the dead the great Shepherd of the sheep through the blood of the eternal covenant, even Jesus our Lord, [21] equip you in every good thing to do His will, working in us that which is pleasing in His sight, through Jesus Christ, to whom be the glory forever and ever. Amen" (Hebrews 13:20-21). This is a complicated sentence. If you have ony read it once, read it again before we go on.

He is asking God to equip us in every good thing to do God's will. We need to pray that same prayer. Then, he says that doing God's will works in us that which is pleasing to God.

God wants loving, obedient service, and that pleases Him. It is that simple. Do we long to please God? In Psalm 40:8, David says, "I delight to do Your will, O my God; Your Law is within my heart." In the hymn "Living for Jesus" (Thomas O. Chisholm) there is a line, "Striving to please Him in all that I do."

These scriptures help us to learn to please Him:

2 Corinthians 5:9-10 "Therefore we also have as our ambition, whether at home or absent, to be pleasing to Him. [10] For we must all appear before the judgment seat of Christ, so that each one may be recompensed for his deeds in the body, according to what he has done, whether good or bad."

Colossians 1:10 "So that you will walk in a manner worthy of the Lord, to please Him in all respects, bearing fruit in every good work and increasing in the knowledge of God."

Hebrews 11:6 "And without faith it is impossible to please Him, for he who comes to God must believe that He is and that He is a rewarder of those who seek Him.

Romans 8:6-8 "For the mind set on the flesh is death, but the mind set on the Spirit is life and peace, [7] because the mind set on the flesh is hostile toward God; for it does not subject itself to the law of God, for it is not even able to do so, [8] and those who are in the flesh cannot please God."

Look at how the apostle Paul described the church at Thessalonica. "Finally then, brethren, we request and exhort you in the Lord Jesus, that as you received from us instruction as to how you ought to walk and please God (just as you actually do walk), that you excel still more" (1 Thessalonians 4:1). This is strong commendation. He is saying, "You are pleasing God. Do it even more!" Let us keep striving to please God, more and more.

The Spirit leads Paul to ask a critical question for us to ponder. He says, "For am I now seeking the favor of men, or of God? Or am I striving to please men? If I were still trying to please men, I would not be a bond-servant of Christ" (Galatians 1:10). Paul had just told them how amazed he was that they had been drawn away from Christ to a different gospel and sternly warns them not to listen to anyone, not even an angel from heaven, who would preach a different gospel. Paul would only preach the gospel of Christ, even if it cost him their friendship (Galatians 4:16). So there is the question: Do we seek to please God or man? Much hinges on our answer to that question, does it not?

For Further Study God wants us to please Him. He is a loving Father that is ready and eager to be pleased. Some people are hard to please, but not God. We can please Him. Find more passages about pleasing God.

PRAY

"Devote yourselves to prayer, keeping alert in it with an attitude of thanksgiving." Colossians 4:2

HOW JESUS PRAYED:

The Lord taught His disciples to pray while He was here on earth, and He teaches us both by word and example.

Jesus prayed without ceasing. At least once he prayed all night. "It was at this time that He went off to the mountain to pray, and He spent the whole night in prayer to God" (Luke 6:12). He prayed under many circumstances. He prayed when He was baptized (Luke 3:21). He blessed the food before the miracle of feeding the five thousand (Mark 6:41). He gave thanks for the bread and the cup at the Last Supper (Matthew 26:26-27). He was on the mountain praying when He was transfigured (Luke 9:29). He prayed on the return of the seventy (Luke 10:21).

Jesus prayed in many places. He prayed beside a grave (John 11:41-42). He prayed on a mountain (Mark 6:46). He frequently sought out secluded places to pray. For instance, once, in the early morning, while it was still dark, Jesus "got up, left the house, and went away to a secluded place, and was praying there" (Mark 1:35). It mentions that He was praying alone in Luke 9:18. He was praying when His disciples asked Him to teach them to pray (Luke 11:1). He prayed as He foretold His death after His triumphal entry into Jerusalem (John 12:27-28). He prayed in anguish in the garden (Luke 22:39-46). Hebrews 5:7 says, "In the days of His flesh, He offered up both prayers and supplications with loud crying and tears to the One able to save Him from death, and He was heard because of His piety." He prayed from the cross (Luke 23:34-46), where He uttered those precious words, "Father, forgive them" (Luke 23:34).

He prayed for a disciple, "Simon, Simon, behold, Satan has demanded permission to sift you like wheat; [32] but I have prayed for you, that your faith may not fail; and you, when once you have turned again, strengthen your brothers" (Luke 22:31-32). He prayed for children (Matthew 19:13). He prayed for his apostles and for us (John 17) that those who believe in Him would be protected, have joy, be sanctified, be filled with the Father's love, truly know His Father, have eternal life, and be one with the Father, the Son, and one another.

Jesus taught about prayer. He taught persistence in prayer in two parables. (Luke 12 and 18). The parables teach us to pray repeatedly as we wait on God and His timing. Persistent prayer is an expression of faith. It shows reliance on God and trust that He is able to deliver. Jesus showed that not all prayers would be answered as we want them. This is a difficult prayer lesson to learn. Even Jesus knew this hard lesson as He cried out to God the Father from Gethsemane, "Yet not as I will, but as You will" (Matthew 26:36-44). The Father knows our needs better than we do, and He will fulfill those needs in His time and in His way.

Jesus sought frequent communion and intimacy with His Father to be strengthened as He walked in the Father's will. He is our perfect example in prayer.

HOW WE PRAY:

When Jesus taught His disciples to pray, He began (Matthew 6:9a), "Pray, then, in this way: 'Our Father who is in heaven.'" What a glorious and humbling thought that we can enter the throne room of heaven, to commune with our Father, the Sovereign ruler of the universe. We do not elevate that thought enough, do we? How dare we approach the Most High God? Hebrews 4:14-16 says that it is because of the great High Priest Jesus that we can "draw near with confidence to the throne of grace, so that we may receive mercy and find grace to help in time of need." As the prophet Daniel said, we approach Him not on account of any merits of our own, but on account of His great compassion. (Daniel 9:18). He is willing and eager to hear us.

Consider exhortations to pray:

1 Thessalonians 5:17 Pray without ceasing.

Philippians 4:6 Be anxious for nothing, but in everything by prayer and supplication with thanksgiving let your requests be made known to God.

Colossians 4:2 Devote yourselves to prayer, keeping alert in it with an attitude of thanksgiving.

James 5:16 The effective prayer of a righteous man can accomplish much.

1 John 5:14-15 This is the confidence which we have before Him, that, if we ask anything according to His will, He hears us. [15] And if we know that He hears us in whatever we ask, we know that we have the requests which we have asked from Him.

It may be that these exhortations have become so familiar to us that they have lost their power on our hearts. What made prayer so important to Daniel that he was willing to go into the lions' den rather than cease praying? (Daniel 6:10). What gave David the faith to lie on the ground all night for a week praying fervently for his child (2 Samuel 12:16-18)? And what of Jonah praying from the belly of the great fish (Jonah 2:1-9)?

If prayer has become ho-hum, how can we renew our hearts with zeal? Begin by pouring out our hearts to God about why we do not feel the need to pray. Let *that* be our prayer. Be honest with Him in our prayers. Focus our thoughts on Him. Again, let that be our prayer. Focus on the Lord, praise Him and thank Him. Rejoice with Him and thank Him for all our good experiences through the day. When a need arises, take it first to God before phoning a friend or spouse.

Then have regular times to pray even if it feels artificial at first. Write down a prayer list. Pray with others. Pray *for* others. Rather than worry over the problems of loved ones, pray for them. Husbands and wives, pray for your family as you part in the morning. When someone leaves our homes, pray for their welfare as they depart. Better yet, pray with them. Consider how John prayed for his beloved "child" Gaius. "Beloved, I pray that in all respects you may prosper and be in good health, just as your soul prospers" (3 John 2).

Nothing can restore our souls like a constant communion with the Lord. That can be our goal today. Start now. It is easy. Point your thoughts to God and share. When you wash dishes, pray. In the car, pray. Folding laundry, mowing the yard, walking or running--pray. He has promised to hear.

For Further Study: Let us think about our prayers. How would we characterize them? Are they personal and meaningful?

Do they include:

--Praise and Worship,
--Thanksgiving,
--Sorrow over sins and resolving to do better,
--Intercession (for others), and
--Petition (for self)?

Can we make our prayers more spiritual, more about God and less about us? Let us thank God that He hears and answers.

BE PURE

"For God has not called us for the purpose of impurity, but in sanctification." 1 Thessalonians 4:7

HOW JESUS IS PURE:

Purity can be defined as "freedom from contamination or defilement." For instance, Ivory soap is advertised as 99 and 44/100% pure. That leaves a miniscule amount of impurities – 56 out of every 10000 parts. Also, pure gold is gold that has been refined with fire to such a degree that all dross has been removed. It is, in essence, all gold, without contamination.

It is sin that contaminates the soul. In Psalm 51:7, David said, "Purify me with hyssop, and I shall be clean; Wash me, and I shall be whiter than snow." Hyssop was a plant that the priests used to apply the blood in ceremonial cleansings. David was using hyssop figuratively to represent his purification from sin.

Hebrews 9:19-22 talks of purification by blood. "For when every commandment had been spoken by Moses to all the people according to the Law, he took the blood of the calves and the goats, with water and scarlet wool and hyssop, and sprinkled both the book itself and all the people, [20] saying, 'This is the blood of the covenant which God commanded you.' [21] And in the same way he sprinkled both the tabernacle and all the vessels of the ministry with the blood."

We read in 1 John 3:3 that Jesus is pure. "And everyone who has this hope fixed on Him purifies himself, just as He is pure." Jesus was pure, not because of cleansing, but because He never contaminated himself with sin. Further on in verse five John says, "You know that He appeared in order to take away sins; and in Him there is no sin." Hebrews 4:15: "For we do not have a high priest who cannot sympathize with our weaknesses, but One who has been tempted in all things as we are, yet without sin."

Why was it so important that Jesus did not sin? The sacrificial lamb had to be without spot or blemish (Exodus 12:5, Leviticus 22:24, Deuteronomy 17:1). Hebrews 9:14: "How much more will the blood of Christ, who through the eternal Spirit offered Himself without blemish to God, cleanse your conscience from dead works to serve the living God?"

The High Priest also had to be pure. The Levitical priests had to undergo purification before they could offer sacrifices (Leviticus 16:32-33). One such example: After the return of the exiles from Babylonia, they rebuilt the temple and observed the Passover. "For the priests and the Levites had purified themselves together; all of them were pure" (Ezra 6:20). Jesus required no purification, because He was never defiled. In Hebrews 7:26, "For it was fitting for us to have such a high priest, holy, innocent, undefiled, separated from sinners and exalted above the heavens."

The sinless life and subsequent resurrection of Jesus overcame Satan. (1 Corinthians 15:56-57). By living a sinless life, Jesus demonstrated complete dominance over sin, and by overcoming every temptation, He demonstrated complete authority over Satan.

Without contamination from sin, Jesus was 100% pure. We thank God that Jesus was willing to live a pure life for us.

HOW WE ARE PURE:

Paul wrote that Jesus "gave Himself for us to redeem us from every lawless deed, and to purify for Himself a people for His own possession, zealous for good deeds" (Titus 2:14). Jesus' sacrifice produced many changes in believers. It saved, redeemed, sanctified, and justified us, just to name a few. Here it says that it "purified" us, and for a special reason—to create for Himself a "people for His own possession." Jesus wanted a pure, uncontaminated people for His own.

The apostle Peter said it this way, "But you are a chosen race, a royal priesthood, a holy nation, a people for God's own possession, so that you may proclaim the excellencies of Him who has called you out of darkness into His marvelous light" (1 Peter 2:9). What a great blessing to be God's special, pure people.

Jesus said in the Sermon on the Mount, "Blessed are the pure in heart, for they shall see God." (Matthew 5:8). Jesus was teaching the Jews about His coming kingdom, so He was talking here about the purification of heart that comes through accepting Him as Lord.

Jesus made us pure, but we are warned to *keep* ourselves pure. John put a condition on our perpetual cleansing. 1 John 1:7 says, "But if we walk in the Light as He Himself is in the Light, we have fellowship with one another, and the blood of Jesus His Son cleanses us from all sin." The apostle Paul warned the young preacher Timothy, "Let no one look down on your youthfulness, but rather in speech, conduct, love, faith and purity, show yourself an example of those who believe" (1 Timothy 4:12). Paul was concerned that the church in Corinth would be led away from its purity. "But I am afraid that, as the serpent deceived Eve by his craftiness, your minds will be led astray from the simplicity and purity of devotion to Christ" (2 Corinthians 11:3).

When we think of impurity, we often think of sexual sin, but Paul is speaking of our pure devotion to Christ. Our service to Him must not contain impurities. Impurity includes all kinds of sin and encompasses any activity, thought, word, or deed that does not conform to God's will for our lives. "God did not call us to be impure, but to live a holy life" (1 Thessalonians 4:7).

For Further Study: Let us consider our own lives. What are ways that we need a purer heart? In kindness? In selflessness? In service? Pray today for strength. *Purer in Heart* is a prayer that may help us to focus our prayer.

Purer in Heart A. Davion (unknown) Public Domain

Purer in heart, O God, Help me to be;
May I devote my life Wholly to Thee.
Watch Thou my wayward feet,
Guide me with counsel sweet;
Purer in heart, Help me to be.

Purer in heart, O God, Help me to be;
Teach me to do Thy will Most lovingly.
Be Thou my friend and guide,
Let me with Thee abide;
Purer in heart, Help me to be.

Purer in heart, O God, Help me to be;
Until Thy holy face One day I see.
Keep me from secret sin,
Reign Thou my soul within;
Purer in heart, Help me to be.

BE QUIET

"Make it your ambition to lead a quiet life." 1 Thessalonians 4:11

HOW JESUS WAS QUIET:

The word "quiet" in the scriptures makes for an interesting study. Its most common definition in English is "free from noise," but a second definition is "state of being calm." The word "quiet" occurs 34 times in the NASB95. In several places it describes a peaceful or calm existence. For instance, in 2 Kings 11:20, after they had put the horrible queen Athaliah to death, it says, "So all the people of the land rejoiced and the city was quiet." Job 20:20 uses quiet to describe an inner calm. "Because he knew no quiet within him, He does not retain anything he desires."

"Silent" is another closely related word. Habakkuk 2:20: "But the LORD is in His holy temple. Let all the earth be silent before Him." Rather than a mere absence of noise, silence here represents the reverence the creation expresses because of His majesty and power (in contrast to the idols Habakkuk had just described). Most of us know the simple, yet awe-inspiring song "The Lord Is in His Holy Temple" based on this verse.

Old Testament prophecies of Jesus use this notion of "quiet" or "silence." Zephaniah 3:17 is one of the most joyful verses of the Old Testament. "The LORD your God is in your midst, a mighty one who will save; he will rejoice over you with gladness; he will quiet you by his love; he will exult over you with loud singing" (ESV). The phrase "he will quiet you by his love" is rendered in some versions as "He will be quiet in His love." Scholars disagree about what this phrase means. Are we made calm by His love as the first would indicate, or has God been quieted or satisfied by the Son's sacrifice? Both statements are true. The main

140

idea is that through the sacrifice of Christ and man's obedience to it, God's wrath is quieted, and He is willing to bring man back to Him.

We read in Mark 4 of a storm so violent that water was filling the boat where Jesus was. Think of the calm that it took for Him to lie asleep. When his frightened disciples woke Him, they asked, "Teacher, do You not care that we are perishing?" Then, He performed the great miracle of quieting the winds and sea. Jesus' reaction was "Why are you afraid? Do you still have no faith?" Faith is what quiets the spirit in the storms of life. In the hymn *Master the Tempest is Raging* (M. Baker), the author captures this metaphor. Consider the words of the chorus:

The winds and the waves shall obey thy will: Peace, be still.
Whether the wrath of the storm-tossed sea
Or demons or men or whatever it be,
No waters can swallow the ship where lies
The Master of ocean and earth and skies.
They all shall sweetly obey thy will: Peace, be still; peace, be still.
They all shall sweetly obey thy will: Peace, peace, be still.

In the storms of life, let us recall the words of Jesus, "Why are you afraid?" Faith in Jesus calms the storms of life.

HOW WE ARE TO BE QUIET:

1 Thessalonians 4:11 teaches, "Make it your ambition to lead a quiet life and attend to your own business and work with your hands, just as we commanded you." To be quiet like Jesus means we live with a peaceful and calm spirit. Notice how Paul

says, "make it your ambition" and then relates three directives: lead a quiet life, mind your own business, and be industrious.

The scriptures teach us to pray for our leaders so that we may lead a "tranquil and quiet life." "First of all, then, I urge that entreaties and prayers, petitions and thanksgivings, be made on behalf of all men, [2] for kings and all who are in authority, so that we may lead a tranquil and quiet life in all godliness and dignity" (1 Timothy 2:1-2). *Vine's* says that quiet in this verse "indicates 'tranquility arising from within,' causing no disturbance to others." It does not mean not talking, per se, but living a peaceful life, not harassing others. Further, he describes a peaceful and quiet life as a godly and dignified life.

1 Peter 3:4 uses the same Greek word for quiet to emphasize that women's adornment should be "the hidden person of the heart, with the imperishable quality of a gentle and quiet spirit, which is precious in the sight of God." A quiet spirit is what is precious in God's sight and that should be our focus. Again, not that we are silent in speech, but that we have a peaceful spirit. As it has been described, like a placid lake. It brings to mind Jesus' words, "Peace, be still" when he calmed the sea.

Philippians 4:5-7: "Let your gentle spirit be known to all men. The Lord is near. [6] Be anxious for nothing, but in everything by prayer and supplication with thanksgiving let your requests be made known to God. [7] And the peace of God, which surpasses all comprehension, will guard your hearts and your minds in Christ Jesus." That is what gives us a quiet spirit. In contrast, we must question the wisdom of over absorbing news and social media that constantly bombard us with doomsday newscasts designed to alarm and upset us. Some seem to think it is their responsibility to keep an ear to the world, but if it causes us to be anxious, then we are violating this passage, and we need to give it up. We cannot solve the world's problems. Our responsibility is to live a quiet life, and we can do this without our regular "fix" of anxiety.

A quiet or calm spirit is a great blessing from God. David says in Psalm 62:1-2, "My soul waits in silence for God only; From Him is my salvation. [2] He only is my rock and my salvation, My stronghold; I shall not be greatly shaken," and for emphasis he repeats the identical claim in verse five. Look what David was facing from his enemies: "How long will you assail a man, That you may murder him, all of you, Like a leaning wall, like a tottering fence?" (Psalm 62:3). But because of his trust in the Lord, David could wait in silence, in calm, for the Lord.

For Further Study: Let us examine our spirits and notice what challenges our "quiet." Find scriptures that encourage us to live a quiet life. Consider why it is that we would choose aggravation and anxiety over a calm and quiet life in Christ.

REJOICE

"I will be glad and rejoice in you; I will sing the praises of your name, O Most High." Psalm 9:2 NIV

HOW JESUS REJOICED:

We do not emphasize enough the rejoicing of Jesus and the Father. Yes, it grieves God that man sins, but He greatly rejoices over man's return to Him. Many prophecies describe the rejoicing of Jesus and the Father over His plan to save man through His Son.

Jeremiah 32:40-42: "I will make an everlasting covenant with them that I will not turn away from them, to do them good; and I will put the fear of Me in their hearts so that they will not turn away from Me. [41] I will rejoice over them to do them good and will faithfully plant them in this land with all My heart and with all My soul. [42] For thus says the Lord, 'Just as I brought all this great disaster on this people, so I am going to bring on them all the good that I am promising them.'"

Zephaniah 3:17 is one of the most joyful verses of the Old Testament. "The LORD your God is in your midst, a mighty one who will save; he will rejoice over you with gladness; he will quiet you by his love; he will exult over you with loud singing." (ESV) Consider the Lord being so joyful over us that He exults over us with loud singing.

Isaiah 62:5: "As the bridegroom rejoices over the bride, So your God will rejoice over you."

Isaiah 11:1-3: "Then a shoot will spring from the stem of Jesse, And a branch from his roots will bear fruit. [2] The Spirit of the Lord will rest on Him, The spirit of wisdom and understanding, The spirit of counsel and strength, The spirit of knowledge and the fear of the Lord. [3] And He will delight in the fear of the Lord."

Psalm 149:4: "For the LORD takes pleasure in His people; He will beautify the afflicted ones with salvation."

Do we ever think about God rejoicing over us? Observe the father's emotion on the return of the son in Luke 15: 22-24: "But the father said to his slaves, 'Quickly bring out the best robe and put it on him, and put a ring on his hand and sandals on his feet; [23]and bring the fattened calf, kill it, and let us eat and celebrate; [24]for this son of mine was dead and has come to life again; he was lost and has been found.' And they began to celebrate." How sweet it is to think of delighting the Lord rather than grieving Him. Let us thank God that it gives Him such delight to forgive and save us.

The writer to the Hebrews speaks of the Lord Jesus as being motivated to carry out His work on the cross of Calvary by the "joy set before Him" (Hebrews 12:2). Thank God for that joy. In John 15:11, after describing to His disciples how they can abide in Him, He says, "These things I have spoken to you so that My joy may be in you, and that your joy may be made full." Then in Jesus' tender prayer for His disciples, He prays, "But now I come to You; and these things I speak in the world so that they may have My joy made full in themselves" (John 17:13). He prayed that His joy would be made full in us. Have we let Jesus' joy fill us? We will see how to do this in the next section.

HOW WE REJOICE:

We are familiar with Paul's exhortations in his letter to the church in Philippi to rejoice. He tells us to rejoice in the Lord always. But how? How do we rejoice in sickness, in loss of loved ones, or in heartaches of any kind? When Paul said rejoice always, he did not mean to be in a state of constant giddiness and unending exuberance. Paul's exhortation is that we can rejoice over our salvation every moment of our lives! We can be filled with the joy of Jesus as He prayed. We can rejoice that God loves us and cares for us every moment. No matter what our outward circumstances are, we can rejoice in the Lord.

Paul is not saying we should rejoice over causes for mourning. When we have cause for mourning, say, the loss of a precious child, we will mourn over that. Remember how David mourned over the illness of his child (2 Samuel 12:16): "David therefore inquired of God for the child; and David fasted and went and lay all night on the ground." But even in our most distraught times, we still have our salvation and the love and care of our great God, and we will rejoice over that always and in all ways.

HYMN

Joy to the World! Isaac Watts (1719) Public Domain

Joy to the world, the Lord is come!
Let earth receive her King;
Let every heart prepare Him room,
And heav'n and nature sing,
And heav'n and nature sing,
And heav'n, and heav'n, and nature sing.

The Lord's coming gives the whole creation joy. What a great thought: "Let every heart prepare Him room." Make room in our hearts for the Lord and rejoice!

Let us read the scriptures for greater inspiration to rejoice:

Psalm 5:11 NIV: "But let all who take refuge in you be glad; let them ever sing for joy. Spread your protection over them, that those who love your name may rejoice in you."

Psalm 9:2 NIV: "I will be glad and rejoice in you; I will sing the praises of your name, O Most High."

Psalm 32:11: "Be glad in the LORD and rejoice, you righteous ones; And shout for joy, all you who are upright in heart."

Romans 12:15: "Rejoice with those who rejoice; mourn with those who mourn."

2 Corinthians 13:11: "Finally, brethren, rejoice! Be made complete, be comforted, be like-minded, live in peace; and the God of love and peace will be with you."

Revelation 19:7: "Let us rejoice and be glad and give the glory to Him."

Acts 5:41: "So they went on their way from the presence of the Council, rejoicing that they had been considered worthy to suffer shame for His name."

Acts 8:39: "When they came up out of the water, the Spirit of the Lord snatched Philip away, and the eunuch no longer saw him, but went on his way rejoicing."

How do we learn to rejoice if that is hard for us? We must focus on our blessings and be thankful. We must pray for joy and believe that we will receive it. We should give up our worries and instead trust in God. We must learn to focus on what we have and not what we lack. If we are unhappy with our job, we must thank God that we have a job to provide for our needs. If we have housework that is drudgery to us, we should thank God for the blessings of a home. We can turn our gloomy thoughts into joyous ones.

For Further Study Many hymns are joyous ones. Find hymns that lift our spirits high.

RESIST TEMPTATION

"Your word I have treasured in my heart, That I may not sin against You." Psalm 119: 11

HOW JESUS RESISTED TEMPTATION:

Temptation is agonizing. There may be sins that we struggle against all our lives. Consider alcoholics or drug addicts that are "clean" for years and then at a dark point give in to the temptation and are back in that black hole. Think of those who struggle with anger, unkindness, or unforgiveness. They may forgive a grievance against another and think they have overcome it, then one day it comes into mind as strongly as before. One of the great blessings of heaven is that temptation will be no more.

Temptation is a trial or enticement where we have the choice to be faithful or unfaithful to God. Jesus is the only one that has resisted every temptation he ever experienced. Hebrews 4:15 says Jesus never sinned even though He was tempted in all points like us. Consider the power of that statement. He was tempted just like us in every way, but He never gave in.

Why was Jesus even willing to undergo temptation? In heaven, He could not be tempted (James 1:13), but Hebrews 2:18 says, "For since He Himself was tempted in that which He has suffered, He is able to come to the aid of those who are tempted." Because of us, He humbled Himself to be tempted. Notice in Matthew 4:1 it says that Jesus was led into the wilderness by the Spirit to be tempted. It was planned and purposed by God.

There Jesus gave us an example of how to resist Satan. Matthew 4:1-11 tells of three temptations. Each time, Jesus resisted and answered with "it is written". Jesus used the Word of God to stand down the devil, referencing Deuteronomy 8:3, 6:16, and 6:13.

Look at Psalm 119:11: "Your word I have treasured in my heart, That I may not sin against You." Jesus also showed us to pray in times of temptation. He prayed fervently in the Garden of Gethsemane before His arrest. Out of concern for what His disciples would face, He commanded them to pray that they may not "enter into temptation."

HOW WE CAN RESIST TEMPTATION:

It is said that death and taxes are the two sure things in life. Well, temptation is another. If Satan will dare to tempt the Son of God, he will have no fear of us. Temptation is sure to come, yet God has given us ways to help us resist. Here are some things we can do:

1) Meditate on His word: Psalms 119:11 says, "I have hidden your word in my heart that I might not sin against you." Hiding the word in our heart means we guard it as a great treasure. It is not that we merely quote some scripture to the devil, and he will run, but that we treasure the word of God and seek with all our hearts to live by it.

2) Pray for strength: Prayer is another powerful way to resist temptation. Jesus told His disciples to watch and pray so that they would not enter into temptation. 2 Thessalonians 3:3 says to pray because "the Lord is faithful, and he will strengthen you and protect you from the evil one."

3) Know our weaknesses: 2 Corinthians 13:5 says, "Test yourselves to see if you are in the faith; examine yourselves!" We must scrutinize our life, take an intense look at our spiritual being. This is not always a pleasant exercise. It takes an honest assessment of our commitment. When David said, "For I know my transgressions," (Psalm 51:3), he is being brutally honest with himself and with God.

4) Run from temptation: Are we over-confident about sin? 1 Corinthians 10:12: "Therefore let him who thinks he stands take heed that he does not fall." Few Christians are going to sin the first time they are tempted by it. If our conscience is pure, it will warn us away. But Satan is going to attack us in different ways and at different times, hoping that we will sear our conscience (1 Timothy 4:1-2). We must work every day to become stronger and closer to God and run away from sin. James 4:7: "Submit yourselves therefore to God. Resist the devil and he will flee from you. "

5) Seek support of other Christians. We have others to help us. Galatians 6:1 tells us that the spiritually strong should help restore those who are caught in sin, but it is even better if we can help one another avoid sin altogether. Likewise, James 5:16 says to confess our temptations to one another and pray for one another. It will make us both stronger. Often, we learn after the fact that a Christian has fought and lost a battle with temptation, and no one in the congregation had any idea.

Remember 1 Corinthians 10:13: "No temptation has overtaken you but such as is common to man; and God is faithful, who will not allow you to be tempted beyond what you are able, but with the temptation will provide the way of escape also, so that you will be able to endure it." The ways of escaping temptations may take many different forms, and we should seek them out. We must take advantage of the escape that the Lord provides and not just passively let ourselves be controlled by Satan. One way that we can do this is by putting on the armor of God (the Armed for Battle lesson, page # 9).

For Further Study: Let us examine our hearts and write down a list of our greatest temptations. Remember we have to be honest with ourselves. Whatever they are, find passages that address those temptations and pray. Trust the Lord to help us overcome. The main thing is to not be indifferent or satisfied with our temptations. Fight the battle, but we don't have to fight it alone!

HYMN

Yield Not to Temptation H. Palmer (1868) Public Domain

Yield not to temptation, for yielding is sin;
Each vict'ry will help you some other to win;
Fight manfully onward, dark passions subdue;
Look ever to Jesus, He will carry you through.

Refrain: Ask the Savior to help you,
Comfort, strengthen, and keep you;
He is willing to aid you, He will carry you through.

Shun evil companions, bad language disdain,
God's name hold in reverence, nor take it in vain;
Be thoughtful and earnest, kindhearted and true;
Look ever to Jesus, He will carry you through.

To him that o'ercometh, God giveth a crown,
Through faith we will conquer, though often cast down;
He who is our Savior, our strength will renew;
Look ever to Jesus, He will carry you through.

SACRIFICE

"Through Him then, let us continually offer up a sacrifice of praise to God, that is, the fruit of lips that give thanks to His name."
Hebrews 13:15

HOW JESUS SACRIFICED:

Webster defines sacrifice as "an act of offering to a deity something precious." No sacrifice more precious has ever been offered than Jesus Christ. Ephesians 5:2 says Jesus gave Himself up for us as an "offering and a sacrifice to God as a fragrant aroma." Jesus did not only sacrifice Himself on the cross; His entire life was a sacrifice. Although He was equal to God, He sacrificed His divine privilege in order to walk this earth as a human and live a perfect life of sacrifice.

Nothing can strengthen our hearts more than meditating on the sacrifice of God and His dear Son for us. Since we are the created and He is the Creator, we understand that we need to sacrifice to Him. But that the Creator would sacrifice for the created is amazing indeed. These verses emphasize that sacrifice.

Hebrews 10:12: "But He, having offered one sacrifice for sins for all time, sat down at the right hand of God."

Hebrews 7:27: "[He] does not need daily, like the other high priests, to offer up sacrifices, first for His own sins and then for the sins of the people, because this He did once for all when He offered up Himself."

John 3 contains much more than the beloved John 3:16. In verses 14-15, Jesus referenced something that had happened hundreds of years earlier. When Israel had complained to Moses about conditions in the wilderness, God sent deadly snakes as punishment. After the people went to Moses for help, he intervened to God, and God relented and instructed Moses to mount an image of a snake on a pole. The scriptures say, "And Moses made a bronze serpent and set it on the standard; and it came about, that if a serpent bit any man, when he looked to the bronze serpent, he lived" (Numbers 21:9).

Now consider Jesus' statement, the context of John 3:16, starting with verse 14. "As Moses lifted up the serpent in the wilderness, even so must the Son of Man be lifted up; [15]so that whoever believes will in Him have eternal life. [16]For God so loved the world, that He gave His only begotten Son, that whoever believes in Him shall not perish, but have eternal life. [17]For God did not send the Son into the world to judge the world, but that the world might be saved through Him." In John 12:32, Jesus identified Himself as the one that would be lifted up. Then John explained that Jesus said this "to indicate the kind of death by which He was to die" (Verse 33).

The wilderness event represents how salvation would be brought through the sacrifice of Jesus Christ. The Israelites' idolatry resulted in their death. In the same way, all people die because of sin (Romans 6:23). The Israelites' only hope was to trust in something beyond themselves and look at the serpent. Our only hope is trusting in something beyond ourselves and look to Jesus (Romans 5:6). And as John tells us, it was because of God's love that the sacrifice was made (John 3:16).

The Jews would have been very familiar with this story. Jesus meant it as evidence of Him as the One sent. What a great sacrifice! How could we ever doubt His love?

HOW WE SACRIFICE:

I Gave My Life for Thee F. Havergal(1859)

I gave My life for thee, My precious blood I shed,
That thou might ransomed be, And raised up from the dead;
I gave, I gave My life for thee, What hast thou giv'n for Me?
I gave, I gave My life for thee, What hast thou giv'n for Me?

My Father's house of light, My glory-circled throne
I left for earthly night, For wand'rings sad and lone;
I left, I left it all for thee, Hast thou left aught for Me?
I left, I left it all for thee, Hast thou left aught for Me?

I suffered much for thee, More than thy tongue can tell,
Of bitt'rest agony, To rescue thee from hell;
I've borne, I've borne it all for thee, What hast thou borne for Me?
I've borne, I've borne it all for thee, What hast thou borne for Me?

And I have brought to thee, Down from My home above,
Salvation full and free, My pardon and My love;
I bring, I bring rich gifts to thee, What hast thou brought to Me?
I bring, I bring rich gifts to thee, What hast thou brought to Me?

This hymn poignantly points out the sacrifice of Jesus, then asks, "What have we done for Him? What have we given for Him? What have we left for Him? What have we borne for Him? What have we brought to Him?" How do we answer those questions? What is our sacrifice to God?

Sacrifice of praise: Romans 11:33-36 says, "Oh, the depth of the riches both of the wisdom and knowledge of God! How unsearchable are His judgments and unfathomable His ways! [34] For who has known the mind of the Lord, or who became His counselor? [35] Or who has first given to Him that it might be paid back to him again? [36] For from Him and through Him and to Him are all things. To Him be the glory forever. Amen." The Lord is worthy of all praise. We could not over-praise Him. The Hebrew writer wrote, "Through Him then, let us continually offer up a sacrifice of praise to God, that is, the fruit of lips that give thanks to His name" (Hebrews 13:15).

Sacrifice of our lives: There is an unfortunate chapter break between Romans 11 and 12. At the end of chapter 11 we read the great praises recorded in the preceding paragraph, and then chapter 12 starts with "Therefore". In other words, because of God's greatness, then something needs to happen. Romans 12:1 reads, "Therefore I urge you, brethren, by the mercies of God, to present your bodies a living and holy sacrifice, acceptable to God, which is your spiritual service of worship." Because of who God is, it is reasonable for us to offer all of ourselves and all of our lives to Him holding nothing back.

Sacrifice of possessions: Generous giving is another New Testament sacrifice. It is another sacrifice the writer of Hebrews says pleases God: "And do not neglect doing good and sharing, for with such sacrifices God is pleased" (Hebrews 13:16).

Sacrifice of our old self: Romans 6:6 says, "Knowing this, that our old self was crucified with Him, in order that our body of sin might be done away with, so that we would no longer be slaves to sin." We have to give up that old familiar way of life, the old self-driven way. We must sacrifice our rights and desires in order to fully obey God.

For Further Study Write out the questions from the hymn "I Gave My Life for Thee" and answer them. Can we use these questions to become more of a sacrifice for Jesus? Let us thank God for His great sacrifice.

SEEK AND SAVE THE LOST

"Go therefore and make disciples of all nations, baptizing them in the name of the Father and of the Son and of the Holy Spirit."
Matthew 28:19

HOW JESUS SAVES:

Jesus summarized His purpose on earth. "'For the Son of Man has come to seek and to save that which was lost" (Luke 19:10). A line in the familiar hymn "Amazing Grace" says, "I once was lost but now am found, was blind but now I see." What does it mean to be spiritually "lost"? It is to have wandered away from God, helpless to find our way back. A hiker may take a wrong turn and be lost. Often search parties will be formed to look for the lost. Jesus is our search party, coming to seek and save us (Luke 19:10).

Isaiah 53:6 says, "All of us like sheep have gone astray, Each of us has turned to his own way. But the Lord has caused the iniquity of us all To fall on Him." When we are spiritually lost, our sin separates us from God, and we are unable to find our way back, but Jesus finds us and returns us to Him.

After Jesus was baptized, fasted, and then tempted, He began his ministry in Capernaum. "From that time Jesus began to preach and say, 'Repent, for the kingdom of heaven is at hand'" (Matthew 4:17). As Jesus went about Galilee teaching in the synagogues and proclaiming the gospel of the kingdom, news spread about Him, and great crowds followed him. We read the great sermon that he preached on the mountain recorded in Matthew 5-7. At its conclusion we are told, "When Jesus had finished these words, the crowds were amazed at His teaching; [29] for He was teaching them as one having authority, and not as their scribes" (Matthew 7:28-29).

Jesus came to save us, but what does He save us from? In Romans 1:18 we read: "For the wrath of God is revealed from heaven against all ungodliness and unrighteousness of men who suppress the truth in unrighteousness." The wrath of God is something that we don't like to think about, yet it is as real as His love. John says in John 3:36: "He who believes in the Son has eternal life; but he who does not obey the Son will not see life, but the wrath of God abides on him." We are saved through our belief and obedience to Jesus. Romans 5:9 reveals, "Much more then, having now been justified by His blood, we shall be saved from the wrath of God through Him." There is the answer to the question: Jesus saves us from the wrath of God.

Jesus has done His part in our salvation. What is our part?
--Believe in Jesus as God's Son (Hebrews 11:6, John 20:31).
--Repent (Regret and turn from) our sins (Luke 13:3, Acts 17:30).
--Confess our faith in Jesus (Romans 10:10, Matthew 10:32).
--Be Baptized (Galatians 3:27, Mark 16:16, Acts 2:38).
--Live faithfully unto death (Revelation 2:10).

In Acts 2 Jews who believed the apostles' teaching were cut to the heart when they realized it was the Messiah that they had crucified. They then asked, "what can we do?" Carefully notice Peter's response. "Repent, and each of you be baptized in the name of Jesus Christ for the forgiveness of your sins; and you will receive the gift of the Holy Spirit." (Acts 2:38). Baptism is said to be "for the remission of sins". Unless we are prepared to say that we are saved without our sins being forgiven, then we must admit that baptism is a condition of salvation. Some do not believe this, even though many scriptures indicate this truth. Let us read a few with an open mind: Acts 22:16; Romans 6:3-4; 1 Corinthians 6:11; 1 Peter 3:21; Acts 8:12-13, 34-38; Acts 16:14-15, 32-33; Acts 18:8. Have we done our part in salvation?

How We Seek and Save the Lost:

Before Jesus left the earth, He commanded His apostles, "Go therefore and make disciples of all nations, baptizing them in the name of the Father and of the Son and of the Holy Spirit" (Matthew 28:19). Through the book of Acts, we can read the history of how this unfolded. The apostles made disciples, then those disciples taught others. Paul described it to Timothy in this way, "The things which you have heard from me in the presence of many witnesses, entrust these to faithful men who will be able to teach others also" (2 Timothy 2:2). Faithful ones teach others and those teach others, and so on, all down the line from then to now.

Telling others about Jesus is not a hard thing. After the woman at the well talked to the Lord, she went back to the town and said to the people, "Come, see a man who told me all the things that I have done; this is the Christ, is it not?" (John 4:28-29). If the Samaritan woman could tell others about Christ, certainly we can. We must not be frightened to combat false doctrine. Denominationalism and religious division have muddled the simple message of the gospel, but the true gospel is still God's power to save (Romans 1:16).

Paul wrote of preaching Christ: "For since in the wisdom of God the world through its wisdom did not come to know God, God was well-pleased through the foolishness of the message preached to save those who believe. [22] For indeed Jews ask for signs and Greeks search for wisdom; [23] but we preach Christ crucified, to Jews a stumbling block and to Gentiles foolishness, [24] but to those who are the called, both Jews and Greeks, Christ the power of God and the wisdom of God" (1 Corinthians 1:21-24). Let us seek the lost and tell them about their Savior to escape the wrath of God.

Let us teach by example and by word. Let us teach our children, friends, co-workers, and neighbors. We may study our Bibles when we sit in a waiting room or at a restaurant. We should make our greetings and conversations include the name of the Lord. We must let others see Christ living in us.

With God as our Helper, we will not quit teaching. If someone rejects our teaching, we will go to another. We are not responsible for others' salvation but for teaching. So we must pray for opportunities to teach and then take those opportunities. And let us pray that our hearts will be eager to teach the lost.

For Further Study Read Luke 15. How much does God love the lost?

HYMN

Seeking the Lost W. Ogden (1886) Public Domain

Seeking the lost, yes, kindly entreating
Wanderers on the mountain astray;
"Come unto Me," His message repeating,
Words of the Master speaking today.

Chorus: Going afar upon the mountain,
Bringing the wand'rer back again, back again,
Into the fold of my Redeemer,
Jesus, the Lamb for sinners slain, for sinners slain.

Seeking the lost and pointing to Jesus
Souls that are weak and hearts that are sore,
Leading them forth in ways of salvation,
Showing the path to life evermore. (Chorus)

Thus would I go on missions of mercy,
Following Christ from day unto day,
Cheering the faint and raising the fallen,
Pointing the lost to Jesus, the Way. (Chorus)

SELF-CONTROL

"Like a city that is broken into and without walls   Is a man who has no control over his spirit." Pro. 25:28

HOW JESUS EXERCISED SELF-CONTROL:

Self-control is defined by Webster as "restraint exercised over one's impulses, emotions, or desires." It is controlling our physical actions, appetites, and desires as well as our thoughts, emotions, and speech. The term "temperance" rather than "self-control" was used in the KJV, but self-control is used about a dozen times in more modern versions. Even though the scriptures do not use the specific word extensively, it is a basic requirement of a godly life, so much so that the apostle Paul spoke about it when he taught the Roman governor Felix. "But some days later Felix arrived with Drusilla, his wife who was a Jewess, and sent for Paul and heard him speak about faith in Christ Jesus. [25] But as he was discussing righteousness, self-control and the judgment to come, Felix became frightened and said, "Go away for the present, and when I find time, I will summon you" (Acts 24:24-25).

Self-control is only effective if it is guided by God's will, so in one sense we could call it "God-controlled". We know what it feels like to control ourselves versus just "letting it fly." We hold our tongue, look away, walk away, and turn the other cheek. We are tempted to do one thing, but we do another because we know it is God's will. We also know what it feels like to give in to our sinful desires.

As always, who could we look to more than Jesus for our example in self-control? The Hebrew writer said of Jesus, "For we do not have a high priest who cannot sympathize with our weaknesses, but One who has been tempted in all things as we are, yet without sin" (Hebrews 4:15). We cannot doubt the enormous self-control that Jesus demonstrated. As God who took on the form of man, Jesus experienced the complete human experience. Taking on flesh, He also took on its temptations and needs, yet mastered them totally. Imagine every temptation that you have experienced in your life and succumbed to—unkind words, selfishness, jealousy, envy—and now imagine that you had *never* given in to any of them. That is the kind of self-control that Jesus demonstrated.

Let us think of just one example: His arrest. Judas came to the garden with a large crowd armed with swords and clubs who had been sent from the chief priests and elders. Judas went to Jesus and kissed Him, the pre-arranged sign that would identify Jesus, and the crowd seized Him. Peter then drew out his sword and struck the slave of the high priest and cut off his ear. But Jesus healed it, told him to put away his sword, and then made an amazing statement: "Or do you think that I cannot appeal to My Father, and He will at once put at My disposal more than twelve legions of angels?" (Matthew 26:53). He was willing to go through this ordeal despite His power to summon those legions of angels.

Then all his disciples fled Him and left Him, and there He stood alone with the soldiers. He knew what was soon to happen, yet He controlled Himself, did not call those angels, and was ready to suffer for you and me.

How We Exercise Self-Control:

The great book of wisdom gives us a profound image of a man without self-control. "Like a city that is broken into and without walls Is a man who has no control over his spirit" (Proverbs 25:28). A great illustration is Jericho. When the famous walls of Jericho fell, the Israelites were able to storm the city.

161

Without self-control, our defenses fall, and sin takes over our hearts.

So how do we learn self-control? In Matthew 16:24, Jesus put it like this: "If anyone wishes to come after Me, he must deny himself, and take up his cross and follow Me." So the first question is, do we truly want to follow the Lord? If we do, we have to deny ourselves. That means turning away from the ways of the "old self" and putting on our new self in Christ (Colossians 3:1-10). It means putting Christ constantly in our thoughts and prayers, believing the Lord's way is the best way, and realizing that we are not only bringing ourselves under our own control, but under the control of Christ as well.

Both the fruit of the Spirit and the Christian virtues (as we call them) contain self-control:

Galatians 5:22-23 "But the fruit of the Spirit is love, joy, peace, patience, kindness, goodness, faithfulness, [23]gentleness, self-control; against such things there is no law."

2 Peter 1:5-9 "Now for this very reason also, applying all diligence, in your faith supply moral excellence, and in your moral excellence, knowledge, [6]and in your knowledge, self-control, and in your self-control, perseverance, and in your perseverance, godliness, [7]and in your godliness, brotherly kindness, and in your brotherly kindness, love. [8]For if these qualities are yours and are increasing, they render you neither useless nor unfruitful in the true knowledge of our Lord Jesus Christ. [9]For he who lacks these qualities is blind or short-sighted, having forgotten his purification from his former sins."

Paul compares it to preparing for athletic competition. "Everyone who competes in the games exercises self-control in all things. They then do it to receive a perishable wreath, but we imperishable. [26]Therefore I run in such a way, as not without aim; I box in such a way, as not beating the air; [27]but I discipline my body and make it my slave, so that, after I have preached to others, I myself will not be disqualified" (1 Corinthians 9:25–27). Learning to rule self is one of the hardest things in life, but it is an essential aspect of becoming like Jesus. Communicating with God is the key to it all.

For Further Study Read Matthew 27 and make a list of all the abuses of Jesus. Think of the self-control that it would have taken for Jesus to endure all this without defending himself. Make another list of your challenges for self-control.

HYMN
HYMN

Have Thine Own Way Lord A. Pollard (1902) Public Domain

Have Thine own way, Lord! Have Thine own way!
Thou art the Potter, I am the clay.
Mold me and make me after Thy will,
While I am waiting, yielded and still.

Have Thine own way, Lord! Have Thine own way!
Search me and try me, Master, today!
Whiter than snow, Lord, wash me just now,
As in Thy presence humbly I bow.

Have Thine own way, Lord! Have Thine own way!
Hold o'er my being absolute sway!
Fill with Thy Spirit till all shall see
Christ only, always, living in me.

SERVE

"It is the Lord Christ whom you serve" Colossians 3:24b

HOW JESUS SERVED:

Jesus, who is the Son of God and the same nature as God, became His Servant and ours as well. Paul writes of Jesus in Philippians 2:6-7: "Who, although He existed in the form of God, did not regard equality with God a thing to be grasped, [7] but emptied Himself, taking the form of a bond-servant, and being made in the likeness of men." Think of the enormous love Jesus demonstrated that He, although equal with God, would become a Servant to those that He created.

Isaiah had prophesied that this Servant of the Lord would come. "Behold, My Servant, whom I uphold; My chosen one in whom My soul delights. I have put My Spirit upon Him" (Isaiah 42:1). When Jesus healed many that followed Him in Matthew 12:17-18, Matthew said that Jesus was fulfilling this prophecy.

Jesus was not a servant in title only, but as a servant, he had much to do for the Father. He went about from place to place healing all manner of diseases, performing all kinds of miracles to demonstrate His deity, and teaching the people as no man had ever taught before (Matthew 7:28-29). Jesus' servanthood involved acts of service based on a heart of selflessness and humility and seeking the good of those whom He served. Jesus did not serve others then grumble about having to do it.

We examined His great act of service of washing His disciples' feet in our lesson on humility (page #85). He gave his

164

apostles an additional lesson on servanthood which is recorded in Mark 10:41-45. When they heard James and John asking to sit on His right and left hand, the other ten disciples became indignant, causing Jesus to intervene. "Calling them to Himself, Jesus said to them, 'You know that those who are recognized as rulers of the Gentiles lord it over them; and their great men exercise authority over them. [43] But it is not this way among you, but whoever wishes to become great among you shall be your servant; [44] and whoever wishes to be first among you shall be slave of all. [45] For even the Son of Man did not come to be served, but to serve, and to give His life a ransom for many.'" Yes, just as He practiced, Jesus taught His disciples that greatness is found in servanthood. That is not how man thinks, is it? Servanthood is not an exalted position to men, but it was to Jesus.

Jesus' greatest service was the redemption and salvation of men. This was the service which was before him when He came, and this is the service He finished. As Isaiah said, "He was pierced through for our transgressions, he was crushed for our iniquities... the Lord has caused the iniquity of us all to fall on him" (Isaiah 53:5,6).

I (David) served in the U.S. Marine Corps from 1962-1966. Many times, when I'm wearing my Marine Corps cover (cap), people will say to me, "Thank you for your service." I always appreciate that, but think of how much we owe Jesus for His service and let us thank Him.

HOW WE ARE TO SERVE:

Jesus both taught and demonstrated that true greatness is found in service. He taught that when we serve the "least of these" we are serving Him. Remember the judgement scene:

"Then the King will say to those on His right, 'Come, you who are blessed of My Father, inherit the kingdom prepared for you from the foundation of the world. [35] For I was hungry, and you gave Me something to eat; I was thirsty, and you gave Me something to drink; I was a stranger, and you invited Me in; [36] naked, and you clothed Me; I was sick, and you visited Me; I was in prison, and you came to Me.' [37] Then the righteous will answer Him, 'Lord, when did we see You hungry, and feed You, or thirsty, and give You something to drink? [38] And when did we see You a stranger, and invite You in, or naked, and clothe You? [39] When did we see You sick, or in prison, and come to You?' [40] The King will answer and say to them, 'Truly I say to you, to the extent that you did it to one of these brothers of Mine, even the least of them, you did it to Me'" (Matthew 25:34-40).

If we were to see the Lord Himself hungry, thirsty, needing lodging, or in prison, we would eagerly do all we could to help Him, would we not? But Jesus desires us to treat everyone just like we would treat Him.

Consider these two encouragements to serve:

Colossians 3:23-24: "Whatever you do, work heartily, as for the Lord rather than for men, [24] knowing that from the Lord you will receive the reward as your inheritance. It is the Lord Christ whom you serve."

1 Peter 4:10: "As each one has received a special gift, employ it in serving one another as good stewards of the manifold grace of God."

Hymn

Servant's Song Anonymous

Make me a servant Lord, make me like you
For you are a servant, make me one, too.
Make me a servant, do what you must do
To make me a servant, make me like you.

To love my brother, to serve like you do.
I humble my spirit, I bow before you.
And through my service, I'll be just like you.
So make me a servant, make me like you.

Open my hands Lord and teach me to share
Open my heart Lord and teach me to care,
For service to others is service to you.
Make me a servant, make me like you.

Look at the phrase from the song: "Open my heart Lord and teach me to care." It may be hard for us to admit, but that's the true challenge, to care enough to serve. Someone might say, "I care, but I am too busy." No, we do not care enough if we are "too busy" to make it our priority. Today, let us search for opportunities to serve like Jesus.

For Further Study Find other passages about service. No study can benefit us more than one that treasures the example of Jesus as a Servant and our need to follow that example.

SHINE

"But if we walk in the Light as He Himself is in the Light, we have fellowship with one another I John 1:17

HOW JESUS SHINES:

We do not fully understand darkness today. Electric lights have fooled us into believing that night is not all that different from day. We seldom experience real darkness with our streetlights and headlights and bright lights in our houses available at the flip of a switch. Many scientists consider electric light as one of history's most influential inventions. In biblical times oil-burning lamps could not fully penetrate the darkness. We should stumble around in the darkness a while to appreciate the metaphor of the Light of the world.

Throughout the scriptures, light and dark represent good and evil respectively. Proverbs 4:19 says, "The way of the wicked is like darkness; They do not know over what they stumble." Psalm 119:105 says, "Your word is a lamp to my feet And a light to my path." Isaiah says, "Woe to those who call evil good, and good evil; Who substitute darkness for light and light for darkness; Who substitute bitter for sweet and sweet for bitter!" (Isaiah 5:20).

After man's sin and until Jesus came, the world was in utter darkness. Jesus said in John 12:46, "I have come as Light into the world, so that everyone who believes in Me will not remain in darkness." We will remain in darkness today if we reject Jesus. When Jesus said, "I am the Light of the world" (John 8:12), He was claiming to be the exclusive source of spiritual light. He went on, "He who follows Me will not walk in the darkness, but will have the

Light of life." The "Light of the world" embodies the light of His Truth, the light of His Word, and the light of eternal Life. Those who perceive the true Light will never walk in spiritual darkness. Thank God for the spiritual Light of the world!

Imagine a dark room. We shine light in to dispel the darkness. Likewise, the Light of Jesus Christ has to be shone into the darkness of sin that engulfs hearts. Jesus says to follow Him, and we will walk in the Light of life. If we do not follow Him, we will not have this light, this truth, and this eternal life. How glorious is the Light.

Other passages that describe Jesus as the light include:

John 3:19 "This is the judgment, that the Light has come into the world, and men loved the darkness rather than the Light, for their deeds were evil."

John 1:4, 9 "In Him was life, and the life was the Light of men... ⁹There was the true Light which, coming into the world, enlightens every man."

1 John 2:8 "On the other hand, I am writing a new commandment to you, which is true in Him and in you, because the darkness is passing away and the true Light is already shining."

2 Corinthians 4:6 "For God, who said, 'Light shall shine out of darkness,' is the One who has shone in our hearts to give the Light of the knowledge of the glory of God in the face of Christ."

How We Shine:

Jesus said, "You are the light of the world. A city set on a hill cannot be hidden; [15] nor does anyone light a lamp and put it under a basket, but on the lampstand, and it gives light to all who are in the house. [16] Let your light shine before men in such a way that they may see your good works and glorify your Father who is in heaven" (Matthew 5:14-16). It would be absurd to light a lamp then put it under a basket; the light is then useless.

We are not the source of light that we shine. We are like the moon that gives light by reflecting the source of the sun, the true light. Jesus tells us to reflect His light all over the world. Jesus is saying, do not hide your light. Shine it where people can see the glory of God.

Paul admonishes in Ephesians 5:8, "You were formerly darkness, but now you are Light in the Lord; walk as children of Light." And in 1 John 1:7, it says, "But if we walk in the Light as He Himself is in the Light, we have fellowship with one another, and the blood of Jesus His Son cleanses us from all sin." Let us live our lives today so that others can see Christ through us!

To encourage us to always be prepared for the coming of the Lord, Paul wrote, "But you, brethren, are not in darkness, that the day would overtake you like a thief; [5] for you are all sons of light and sons of day. We are not of night nor of darkness; [6] so then let us not sleep as others do but let us be alert and sober" (1 Thessalonians 5:4-6).

Peter described it beautifully when he said, "But you are a chosen race, a royal priest hood, a holy nation, a people for God's own possession, so that you may proclaim the excellencies of Him who has called you out of darkness into His marvelous light" (1 Peter 2:9).

For Further Study Consider our walk in the "sunlight of love". Make a list of ways that we can shine for Jesus today.

HYMN

Heavenly Sunlight H. Zelley (1899) Public Domain

Walking in sunlight, all of my journey,
over the mountains, through the deep vale;
Jesus has said, "I'll never forsake thee,"
promise divine that never can fail.

Refrain: Heavenly sunlight, heavenly sunlight,
flooding my soul with glory divine:
hallelujah, I am rejoicing,
singing His praises, Jesus is mine.

Shadows around me, shadows above me,
never conceal my Savior and Guide;
He is the light, in Him is no darkness;
ever I'm walking close to His side. [Refrain]

In the bright sunlight, ever rejoicing,
pressing my way to mansions above;
singing His praises gladly I'm walking,
walking in sunlight, sunlight of love. [Refrain]

SING

"O come, let us sing for joy to the Lord, Let us shout joyfully to the rock of our salvation." Psalm 95:1

HOW JESUS SANG:

There is not a lot in the scriptures about Jesus singing, but what is there is quite noteworthy. Shortly before His arrest Jesus shared His last Passover meal with His twelve apostles where He instituted a new memorial that we know as the Lord's Supper. Both Matthew and Mark say that they then sang a hymn before going out to the Mount of Olives (Matthew 26:30; Mark 14:26). The scriptures do not tell us what the hymn was, but Jewish scholars say that Psalm 118 was customarily sung at the end of the Passover meal.

We seldom think of Jesus and His apostles singing psalms together, but singing was an important part of worship in the Old Testament times. We read of instances where the congregation would spontaneously break out in songs of praise, for instance, Moses' great song of praise in Exodus 15. The Israelites had been terrified, finding themselves wedged up against the sea with the Egyptian army in hot pursuit. After the Lord saved them by the parting of the sea, the scriptures say, "They believed in the LORD and in His servant Moses." Immediately following, it says, "Then Moses and the sons of Israel sang this song to the LORD." Consider the joy and relief that they must have felt after going through such an ordeal. The first of the song reads, "I will sing to the LORD, for He is highly exalted; The horse and its rider He has hurled into the sea.[2] The LORD is my strength and song, And He has become my salvation; This is my God, and I will praise Him; My father's God, and I will extol Him.[3] The LORD is a warrior; The LORD is His name.[4] Pharaoh's chariots and his army He has cast into the sea; And the choicest of his officers are drowned in the Red Sea."

Miriam and the women likewise sang praises: "Sing to the Lord, for He is highly exalted; The horse and his rider He has hurled into the sea" (Exodus 15:20-21).

Since the Psalms was the hymnbook of the Israelites, it is, as we would expect, full of singing. The word sing is found 84 times in the Psalms. Many are joyful praise and thanksgivings, yet many also contain lament and deep regret. It is believed by many scholars that the Psalms of Ascent (Psalms 120-134) would be sung as they journeyed to Jerusalem for the feasts. We should recognize that Jesus often would have been surrounded by singing to God.

Hebrews 2:11-12 also talks about Jesus singing, but in a very different context. "For both He who sanctifies and those who are sanctified are all from one Father; for which reason He is not ashamed to call them brethren, [12] saying, 'I will proclaim Your name to My brethren, In the midst of the congregation I will sing Your praise.'" The Hebrew writer here quotes Psalms 22:22 as part of his evidence of our relationship with Jesus.

What a great thought: that Jesus is joining us as our Brother in singing praise to the Father.

HOW WE SING:

A line from the hymn "The New Song," (J.R. Baxter, Jr.) reads, "It thrills my soul to hear the songs of praise, we mortals sing below." Psalms 95:1-2 says, "O come, let us sing for joy to the Lord, Let us shout joyfully to the rock of our salvation. [2] Let us come before His presence with thanksgiving, Let us shout joyfully to Him with psalms." Yes, that is a soul that is thrilled. Think of thrilling our souls with song.

Singing can help us even when we are going through hard times. In Acts 16:25, Paul and Silas were in prison, and at about midnight, they were praying and singing hymns of praise to God. They could not have been jubilant over being imprisoned, but they raised their hearts together to God in song. James says in 5:13, "Is anyone among you suffering? Then he must pray. Is anyone cheerful? He is to sing praises." Singing is fitting for those who are cheerful, and during a time of suffering can likewise relieve sorrows.

Colossians 3:16 is one of our "singing" verses, but it really needs to be taken in its context starting with verse 12. "So, as those who have been chosen of God, holy and beloved, put on a heart of compassion, kindness, humility, gentleness and patience; [13] bearing with one another, and forgiving each other, whoever has a complaint against anyone; just as the Lord forgave you, so also should you. [14] Beyond all these things put on love, which is the perfect bond of unity. [15] Let the peace of Christ rule in your hearts, to which indeed you were called in one body; and be thankful." Now notice the next verse. "Let the word of Christ richly dwell within you, with all wisdom, teaching and admonishing one another with psalms and hymns and spiritual songs, singing with thankfulness in your hearts to God." This whole text deals with our love and devotion to one another. It does a disservice to the passage and to our lives to ignore the "one another" aspect of singing. Let us consider this beautiful description of what we share with brethren when we raise our voices together in song.

For Further Study Singing is a way to express our emotions to God and to one another. Make a list of songs that are especially meaningful to you. Do a search for "sing" and study the passages that encourage us to sing. Let us renew our joy of sharing with brethren in song.

174

HYMN

The New Song J. Baxter (1926) Public Domain

It thrills my soul to hear the songs of praise, We mortals sing below,
And tho' it takes the parting of the ways, Yet I must onward go;
I hope to hear thru'out unnumbered days, The song earth cannot
know, They sing in heav'n a new song, of Moses and the Lamb.

The greatest joy that I have ever known, Is praising Him in song, I
know some day when I have older grown, My voice will not be
strong; But if good seed for Jesus I have sown, With angels I'll
belong, They sing in heav'n a new song, of Moses and the Lamb.

The sweetest song that earth can ever boast, Was sung when Christ
was born, Yet He who walked the Galilean coast, Sometimes was
sad forlorn; He left the earth to send the Holy Ghost, To guide us
till that morn, They sing in heav'n a new song, of Moses and the
Lamb.

Chorus: I want to hear the angels singing, To bid me welcome to
mansions bright and fair; I want to hear the glad harps ringing, with
voices blending rich and rare; I want to see the Master bringing, A
precious life crown that I may own and wear; I want to hear that
mighty chorus sweetly sing, I want to hear that mighty chorus
sweetly sing, I want to hear that mighty chorus sweetly sing, To
hear it swell and ring.

175

BE STRONG

"Seek the LORD and His strength; Seek His face continually"
1 Chronicles 16:11

HOW JESUS IS STRONG:

Isaiah 40:28-29 describes the strength of God. "Do you not know? Have you not heard? The Everlasting God, the Lord, the Creator of the ends of the earth Does not become weary or tired. His understanding is inscrutable.[29] He gives strength to the weary, And to him who lacks might He increases power."

David says in Psalms 68:34-35, "Ascribe strength to God; His majesty is over Israel And His strength is in the skies. [35] O God, *You are* awesome from Your sanctuary. The God of Israel Himself gives strength and power to the people. Blessed be God!"

Proverbs 18:10 says, "The name of the Lord is a strong tower: the righteous runs into it and is safe." We are told that God is our refuge and strength (Psalm 46:1), our hiding place (Psalm 32:7), and a shelter in the time of storm (Isaiah 25:4). God is all powerful and has the strength to do anything He wants.

We read of the great strong man Samson in Judges 13-16, but there is no evidence that Jesus chose to have that kind of physical strength, even though He demonstrated His power through signs and miracles. He calmed the storm with just the words, "Peace, be still." He healed the sick and raised the dead. And the ultimate show of strength was His own resurrection, never to die again. "But God raised Him up again, putting an end to the agony of death, since it was impossible for Him to be held in its power" (Acts 2:24).

176

In Ephesians 1:18 the apostle Paul prays that they may know "what is the surpassing greatness of His power toward us who believe." Do *we* know the greatness of His power toward us? Do we trust it and call on it?

Continuing our reading in Ephesians 1:19b-23: "These are in accordance with the working of the strength of His might [20] which He brought about in Christ, when He raised Him from the dead and seated Him at His right hand in the heavenly places…" God's power raised Jesus from the dead and then gave Him power. "…far above all rule and authority and power and dominion, and every name that is named, not only in this age but also in the one to come. [22] And He put all things in subjection under His feet and gave Him as head over all things to the church, [23] which is His body, the fullness of Him who fills all in all." Everything is in subjection to Jesus. He has power over all.

Jesus now reigns at the "right hand" of God. Rather than a physical location, the "right hand" represents power. Placing Jesus at this symbolic location implies Christ's supremacy and authority. This symbol was referenced frequently in the New Testament: predicted by Jesus in Luke 22:69, preached by Peter in Acts 2:33 and 5:31, seen by Stephen in Acts 7:55-56, used by Paul in Romans 8:34 and Colossians 3:1, and found in Hebrews 1:3; 10:12; 12:2 and also in 1 Peter 3:22.

How strong is Jesus? He controls the whole universe.

HOW WE ARE STRONG:

We often hear in prayers in the church that we are weak, and in one sense this is true. Without God, we are weak. But we do not have to be weak, because with God, we are strong.

177

Let us be strengthened by God's promises. "Do not fear, for I am with you; Do not anxiously look about you, for I am your God. I will strengthen you, surely I will help you, Surely I will uphold you with My righteous right hand" (Isaiah 41:10).

Romans 5:6 shows how God will make us strong. "For while we were still helpless, at the right time Christ died for the ungodly." We were helpless to save ourselves from sin. We were utterly weak. But we are no longer helpless if we have put on Christ.

In a scripture that is often misunderstood, the apostle Paul talks about the strength that God gives (Philippians 4:11-13). He says, "Not that I speak from want, for I have learned to be content in whatever circumstances I am. ^{12} I know how to get along with humble means, and I also know how to live in prosperity; in any and every circumstance I have learned the secret of being filled and going hungry, both of having abundance and suffering need." Then he says, "I can do all things through Him who strengthens me." Paul first describes all the persecutions he has gone through. Then he says he can endure all of this through the strength that Christ provides. This is the meaning of "I can do all things." With God's help, Paul could endure whatever came about.

We also can endure all things through the strength that Christ provides. Remember when God would not remove Paul's "thorn in the flesh" even after Paul prayed repeatedly? Look at God's answer to Paul in 2 Corinthians 12:9-10. "'My grace is sufficient for you, for power is perfected in weakness.' Most gladly, therefore, I will rather boast about my weaknesses, so that the power of Christ may dwell in me." When we suffer, if God does not remove the source of our suffering, it is our opportunity to let the power of Christ dwell in us. Let us learn to say, "Thy grace is sufficient for me."

David said in 1 Chronicles 16:11, "Seek the LORD and His strength; Seek His face continually." We must seek the strength of

God and use it to do good—to build our character, to teach the lost, to avoid temptation, and to become more like Him.

For Further Study Find every scripture that you can about the strength of God and the strength He gives to us. Some pray, "We are weak and sinful." But do we have to be weak and sinful? Rather, we can thank God and praise Him for the strength He gives.

HYMN

We Have an Anchor P. Owens (Unknown) Public Domain

Will your anchor hold in the storms of life,
when the clouds unfold their wings of strife?
When the strong tides lift, and the cables strain,
will your anchor drift, or firm remain?

Refrain: We have an anchor that keeps the soul
steadfast and sure while the billows roll;
fastened to the Rock which cannot move,
grounded firm and deep in the Savior's love!

It is safely moored, 'twill the storms withstand,
For 'tis well secured by the Savior's hand
And the cables passed from His heart to mine,
can defy the blast through strength divine. [Refrain]

SUBMIT

"Submit therefore to God." James 4:7

HOW JESUS SUBMITTED:

Submission is an attitude that says, "I will obey." It means to rank yourself under, be in subjection to, or obey. When Hagar fled from Sarai, the angel told her to return and "submit yourself to her authority" (Genesis 16:9). When the angel came to tell the virgin Mary that she was to bear the Son of God by the Holy Spirit (Luke 1:38), Mary said, "Behold, the bondslave of the Lord; may it be done to me according to your word." What a great statement of submission to God's will.

In Philippians 2:5-7, we read of Jesus' submission. "Have this attitude in yourselves which was also in Christ Jesus, [6]who, although He existed in the form of God, did not regard equality with God a thing to be grasped, [7]but emptied Himself, taking the form of a bond-servant, and being made in the likeness of men. [8]Being found in appearance as a man, He humbled Himself by becoming obedient to the point of death, even death on a cross." Jesus was equal with God but submitted to becoming a man. Every day of Christ's life as a man was a day of submission, even to the point of death.

1 Peter 2:21-24 tells of Christ's ultimate act of submission. "For you have been called for this purpose, since Christ also suffered for you, leaving you an example for you to follow in His steps, [22]who committed no sin, nor was any deceit found in His mouth; [23]and while being reviled, He did not revile in return; while suffering, He uttered no threats, but kept entrusting Himself to Him who judges righteously; [24]and He Himself bore our sins in His

body on the cross, so that we might die to sin and live to righteousness; for by His wounds you were healed."

Jesus also taught submission to human governments with His coin lesson (give to Caesar what is Caesar's, Matthew 22:21). But to whom did Jesus refuse submission? We read of Satan's great failure in the desert to bring Jesus into submission (Matthew 4:1-11). We also read that even though Satan tempted Jesus in every way that we are, He did not sin (Heb. 4:15).

Jesus lived His whole life in submission to the Father, we never see one word or act of rebellion to the Father. But the cross is history's supreme act of submission. It is also the supreme challenge of all time, the supreme conquering of all time, and the supreme act of love of all time. That God the Son would *willingly submit* to the humiliation and pain of the cross for us is the supreme act of history. All of history centers around that act and His subsequent resurrection from the dead. How wonderful to read of it today!

HOW WE SUBMIT:

James 4:7 says, "Submit therefore to God." Submission is not always easy, but if we believe in God and His love, it will become easier as we seek His will for us.

Submission is the opposite of rebellion. The children of Israel were often condemned for a rebellious spirit. As David described them: "A stubborn and rebellious generation, A generation that did not prepare its heart And whose spirit was not faithful to God" (Psalm 78:8). This passage shows us how to develop a spirit of submission—prepare our hearts. Submission requires a humble heart. A humble heart recognizes that God's way, not ours, is the best way.

181

1 Peter 5:6 tells us, "Therefore humble yourselves under the mighty hand of God, that He may exalt you at the proper time." Submission is letting God lead us in His way. Have you ever had a dog on a leash that did not want to let you lead him? He is often interested in all the things around him and stops to explore, or he just wants to go *his* way and not be dominated. You have to keep tugging on the leash, sometimes almost dragging him. That is not submission, is it?

Submission is a process of surrendering our own will to that of our Father's. The un-submissive dog on the leash must be trained to follow the lead of its owner. In the same way, we must train our hearts to submit to God. Having a humble and submissive heart is a choice we make. When we find ourselves struggling with submission, seeking our will rather than God's, we need to pray to God for a humble and submissive heart.

Not only are we to submit to God, but the scriptures also tell us of others to whom we should submit:

Ephesians 5:21 Be subject to one another in the fear of Christ.

Ephesians 5:24 But as the church is subject to Christ, so also the wives ought to be to their husbands in everything.

Hebrews 13:17 Obey your leaders [church elders] and submit to them, for they keep watch over your souls as those who will give an account. Let them do this with joy and not with grief, for this would be unprofitable for you.

Romans 13:1 Every person is to be in subjection to the governing authorities. For there is no authority except from God, and those which exist are established by God.

For Further Study Make a list of people in the Bible who show great submission to God's will.

HYMN

Hymn He Leadeth Me: O Blessed Thought! J. Gilmore(1862)
Public Domain

He leadeth me: O blessed thought!
O words with heavenly comfort fraught!
Whate'er I do, where'er I be,
still 'tis God's hand that leadeth me.

Refrain: He leadeth me, he leadeth me;
by his own hand he leadeth me:
his faithful follower I would be, for by his hand he leadeth me.

Sometimes mid scenes of deepest gloom,
sometimes where Eden's flowers bloom,
by waters calm, o'er troubled sea,
still 'tis God's hand that leadeth me. Refrain

And when my task on earth is done,
when, by thy grace, the victory's won,
e'en death's cold wave I will not flee,
since God through Jordan leadeth me. Refrain

BE THANKFUL

"Give thanks to the LORD, for He is good, For His lovingkindness is everlasting." Psalm 136:1

HOW JESUS WAS THANKFUL:

Giving thanks stems from a grateful heart. Webster's defines gratitude as "the quality of being thankful; readiness to show appreciation for and to return kindness." *True* gratitude is a very emotional experience. Consider receiving a great gift for which we feel highly unworthy; a gift that is an honor to own, perhaps an honor even to hold. That comes close to describing what it means to be grateful. In Romans 6:23, Paul described eternal life in Christ Jesus our Lord as "the free gift of God." What gratitude should swell within us when we read these words. How grateful we are when we think of God's great gifts to us.

We found eight times in the scriptures where Jesus gave thanks to the Father. Several of these involve giving thanks for food. Perhaps food seems the simplest thing on earth, easily taken for granted. Most of us have it in abundance. When Moses described the Promised Land that the Israelites would enter as, "a land of wheat and barley, of vines and fig trees and pomegranates, a land of olive oil and honey; a land where you will eat food without scarcity," he said, "When you have eaten and are satisfied, praise the LORD your God for the good land he has given you" (Deuteronomy 8:8-10). All our provisions, great or small, come from the Father. Jesus recognized this and was thankful.

Jesus gave thanks for seven loaves and a few little fishes that fed four thousand people (Mark 8:6). He gave thanks for five loaves and two fishes and fed five thousand (Matthew 14:19). He gave thanks for food with two disciples in Emmaus (Luke 24:30). This thanksgiving for food is recorded often enough for us that we can conclude that it was a regular practice of our Lord.

In addition to giving thanks for food, other thanksgivings of Jesus are recorded for us. When he was at the tomb of Lazarus, he told the people to roll away the stone from the tomb and then prayed, "Father, I thank You that You have heard Me." Then He said, "I knew that You always hear Me; but because of the people standing around I said it, so that they may believe that You sent Me" (John 11:41-42). Do we thank God for hearing our prayers?

In Matthew 11:20, Jesus prayed, "I thank You, Father, Lord of heaven and earth, that You have hidden these things from the wise and prudent and have revealed them to babes." Jesus is expressing gratitude for the humble ones who accept Him. This is similar to what Paul said in 1 Corinthians 1:21: "For since in the wisdom of God the world through its wisdom did not come to know God, God was well-pleased through the foolishness of the message preached to save those who believe."

When Christ instituted His memorial supper with the disciples, He gave thanks (Luke 22:17,19), yet it was more than thanks for food and drink. The bread represents His body that is to be broken; the cup represents His blood that is to be shed. So He was thanking God for symbols of his impending death that would save mankind. We too thank God for this memorial, for as Paul said, "For as often as you eat this bread and drink the cup, you proclaim the Lord's death until He comes" (1 Corinthians 11:26).

HOW WE GIVE THANKS:

When we were children we were taught to say please and thank you. When we requested or received any kind of gift, we were asked, "Now what do you say?" It was simply considered good manners. Saying please shows that we do not presume upon another to favor us, and thank you expresses gratitude that the other person *has* favored us. What a good practice it is to train children to express these thoughts, but we must be careful that it does not make the giving of thanks perfunctory.

Yesterday, as we were preparing this lesson, we heard someone say, "I am privileged to thank you." What a marvelous thought! How humbling it is to bow before the great King to accept our gift of eternal life from Him. What a privilege it is to thank Him. Four times in the great Psalm 136 the psalmist said, "Give thanks to the LORD, for His lovingkindness is everlasting." Is this what we neglect the most: Thanking God for His goodness towards us? Consider:

Psalm 7:17 "I will give thanks to the LORD according to His righteousness And will sing praise to the name of the LORD Most High."

Psalm 35:18 "I will give You thanks in the great congregation; I will praise You among a mighty throng."

Psalm 105:1 "Oh give thanks to the LORD, call upon His name; Make known His deeds among the peoples."

Psalm 119:62 "At midnight I shall rise to give thanks to You Because of Your righteous ordinances."

Psalm 138:2 "I will bow down toward Your holy temple And give thanks to Your name for Your lovingkindness and Your truth; For You have magnified Your word according to all Your name."

Examples and admonitions from the New Testament include:

1 Corinthians 1:4 "I thank my God always concerning you for the grace of God which was given you in Christ Jesus."

2 Corinthians 1:11 "Then many will give thanks on our behalf for the gracious favor granted us in answer to the prayers of many."

Ephesians 5:20 "Always giving thanks for all things in the name of our Lord Jesus Christ to God, even the Father."

Colossians 3:15, 17 "And let the peace of Christ rule in your hearts, to which indeed you were called in one body; and be thankful.[17] Whatever you do in word or deed, do all in the name of the Lord Jesus, giving thanks through Him to God the Father."

1 Thessalonians 5:18 "In everything give thanks; for this is God's will for you in Christ Jesus."

Let us pray for a grateful heart. Grateful hearts do not complain. They are thankful for all they have. Be thankful for everything: our car (imagine walking everywhere we go), the washing machine (try doing the laundry without it), for hot water (try a cold shower). Gratitude will replace complaining and discontentment.

Let us thank our husband or wife for all he or she does for our family. Let us thank our children for their obedience. Let us thank our parents for rearing us. Let us thank our congregation of God's people for their encouragement. Let us thank the elderly for their good example. Let us thank the young for their faithfulness in spite of many temptations in their world. Let us thank the young mothers and fathers for their determination to raise their children in the Lord. Let us thank everyone who gives us any service.

For Further Study: Do we find ourselves complaining rather than being grateful? We can change that. What about our health? Can we be grateful for the measure of health that we do have? Find people in the scriptures that showed gratitude. When we start to complain, thank God instead!

BE TRUE

"And we know that the Son of God has come, and has given us understanding so that we may know Him who is true." I John 5:20

HOW JESUS IS TRUE:

John 1:7-9 illustrates the meaning of "true" that we want to emphasize here. First speaking of John the Baptist, he writes, "He came as a witness, to testify about the Light, so that all might believe through him. He was not the Light, but he came to testify about the Light." Then about Jesus, John says, "There was the true Light which, coming into the world, enlightens every man." True here (Strong's #228) means real and genuine, authentic. "True" gives greater emphasis to the Light. John could have just said, "He is the Light," but to say He is the "true" Light emphasizes that He is light in every respect. Sometimes we might say, "She is a true Christian." We mean that she does not just call herself a Christian, but she is a genuine and authentic Christian.

Jesus uses the same word describing Himself. In John 6, after He had fed the multitude, the people sought another sign from Him, saying, "Our fathers ate the manna in the wilderness; as it is written, 'He gave them bread out of heaven to eat.'" Jesus then calls Himself the "true bread." "Truly, truly, I say to you, it is not Moses who has given you the bread out of heaven, but it is My Father who gives you the true bread out of heaven." Then Jesus made the great claim, "I am the bread of life; he who comes to Me will not hunger, and he who believes in Me will never thirst." Jesus, the true bread, is much more valuable than earthly bread. Earthly bread sustains earthly life. Jesus is claiming that He is our true sustenance, one that gives spiritual life. Similarly, Jesus later describes Himself as the true vine in John 15:1: "I am the true vine, and My Father is the vinedresser." This is also a life-giving metaphor, and through it, Jesus is claiming a special relationship both to the Father and to His disciples (the branches). Life comes to the branches through the true vine, Jesus.

Another interesting use of "true" is found in Hebrews 8:2: the "true" tabernacle. *Vine's* says, "not that the wilderness tabernacle was false, but that it was a weak and earthly copy of the heavenly." Luke 16:11 carries a similar meaning when Luke contrasts earthly wealth with "true riches." Again, it is not "true riches" versus "false riches," but the "true riches" are more significant and important riches.

Paul said of Christians that they "had turned to God from idols to serve a living and true God" (1 Thessalonians 1:9). Idol worship stands in stark contrast to worship of the true God. The one true God is God through and through. The one true God wants to be known by man and has revealed His power and glory through His Son, who is full of glory, grace, and truth (John 1:14). The one true God loves us and gave His Son for us (John 3:16).

In 1 John 5:20, John emphasizes over and over the trueness of God. "And we know that the Son of God has come and has given us understanding so that we may know Him who is true; and we are in Him who is true, in His Son Jesus Christ." Thank God that Jesus came so that we might know Him who is true.

How We Are To Be True:

Hebrews 10:21-22 tells us clearly how we are to be true. "And since we have a great priest over the house of God, [22] let us draw near with a sincere heart in full assurance of faith, having our hearts sprinkled clean from an evil conscience and our bodies washed with pure water." The word translated "sincere" here is the same Greek word that we discussed earlier for "true." This sincere or true heart is real and genuine. And those with a sincere or true heart are beckoned to draw near to God. God

189

promises a new heart through Christ. "Moreover, I will give you a new heart and put a new spirit within you; and I will remove the heart of stone from your flesh and give you a heart of flesh" (Ezekiel 36:26). With this new, true heart, we draw near to God. This new heart has His new law written on it. "'This is the covenant I will make with the people of Israel after that time,' declares the Lord. "I will put my law in their minds and write it on their hearts. I will be their God, and they will be my people'" (Jeremiah 31:33).

There is a vast difference between people who merely call themselves Christians and genuine, sincere Christians. Christian living involves a transformation of our whole lives out of gratitude to God. A true Christian will have an overarching goal to live like Jesus. "He who says he abides in Him ought himself also to walk just as He walked" (1 John 2:6). A true Christian's life will be deeply rooted in the example of the Messiah. Do we love the Lord and others with all our might? (Mark 12:30-31). Do we look in faith to Him, realizing our total dependence on Him? (Psalm 37:5). Do we abide in Him and practice righteousness? (1 John 2:28-29). Do we demonstrate the fruit of the spirit? (Galatians 5:22-23).

Living as a true Christian is a joy and privilege, but it takes effort. We thank God for His grace as we walk in the footsteps of Jesus on our path to heaven.

For Further Study While reading the hymn below, try to really think about the deep meaning of its words. Find other hymns that we've sung many times and study them to try to see a deeper meaning that you may have missed. Also, do a word study of "true."

HYMN True-hearted, Whole-hearted F. Havergal (1878) Public
Domain

True-hearted, whole-hearted, faithful and loyal,
King of our lives, by Thy grace we will be;
Under the standard exalted and royal,
Strong in Thy strength we will battle for Thee.

Refrain: Peal out the watchword! silence it never!
Song of our spirits, rejoicing and free;
Peal out the watchword! loyal forever,
King of our lives, by Thy grace we will be.

True-hearted, whole-hearted, fullest allegiance
Yielding henceforth to our glorious King;
Valiant endeavor and loving obedience,
Freely and joyously now would we bring. (Refrain)

True-hearted, whole-hearted, Saviour all-glorious!
Take Thy great power and reign there alone,
Over our wills and affections victorious,
Freely surrendered and wholly Thine own. (Refrain)

WALK

"Therefore I, the prisoner of the Lord, implore you to walk in a manner worthy of the calling with which you have been called. " Ephesians 4:1

HOW JESUS WALKED:

In 1 John 2:6, John says, "The one who says he abides in Him ought himself to walk in the same manner as He walked." The scriptures often use the term "walking" to represent living by God's principles and abiding in a constant relationship with the Father. It is said that Enoch "walked with God; and he was not, for God took him" (Genesis 5:24). Noah walked with God (Genesis 6:9), and God said to Abraham, "I am God Almighty; Walk before Me, and be blameless" (Genesis 17:1). David declared, "For Your lovingkindness is before my eyes, And I have walked in Your truth" (Psalm 26:3). This walk is not an infrequent stroll with God, but a constant abiding.

So how did Jesus walk? He walked in perfect unbroken fellowship with His Father. That is the "oneness" that we talked about in the lesson on being one (page #117). There was not a moment that Jesus was walking away from the Father. When Jesus walked in fellowship, He was walking in complete obedience and submission (Philippians 2:8 and Romans 5:19). Jesus also walked in perfect love. He walked in perfect humility and in perfect holiness. Every positive attribute that we can think of, Jesus walked in perfection. But we must not forget that the real import of "walking" is with whom we are walking.

Another sense in which God walks with us is described in Leviticus 26:12. God promised the new nation of Israel that He would "walk among you and be your God, and you shall be My people." He is promising to bless them with immeasurable

192

blessings. The apostle Paul quoted this promise in 2 Corinthians 6:16 to demonstrate that it is also true for those who come to God through faith in Christ. He says, "For we are the temple of the living God; just as God said, 'I will live with them and walk among them, and I will be their God, and they will be my people.'"

God will walk with the faithful in Christ. For the faithful, He is not a faraway God. He is right here walking with us. He tells us that if we draw close to Him, He will draw close to us (James 4:8). Thank you, Lord.

HOW WE WALK:

No, we cannot walk in perfection as Jesus walked, but as 1 John 1:7 says, "But if we walk in the light, as He is in the light, we have fellowship with one another, and the blood of Jesus His Son cleanses us from all sin."

Some of the ways that we walk with God like Jesus did:

In love, Ephesians 5:2 "And walk in love, just as Christ also loved you and gave Himself up for us, an offering and a sacrifice to God as a fragrant aroma."

By the Spirit, Galatians 5:16 "So I say, walk by the Spirit, and you will not carry out the desires of the flesh."

In obedience, 2 John 1:6 "And this is love, that we walk according to His commandments. This is the commandment, just as you have heard from the beginning, that you should walk in it."

In the truth, 3 John 3 "For I was very glad when brethren came and testified to your truth, that is, how you are walking in truth."

In humility, Micah 6:8 "He has told you, O man, what is good; And what does the LORD require of you But to do justice, to love kindness, And to walk humbly with your God?"

Blameless, Proverbs 28:18 "He who walks blamelessly will be delivered, But he who is crooked will fall all at once."

In wisdom, Proverbs 28:26 "He who trusts in his own heart is a fool, But he who walks wisely will be delivered."

Worthy, Colossians 1:10-11 "So that you will walk in a manner worthy of the Lord, to please Him in all respects, bearing fruit in every good work and increasing in the knowledge of God, strengthened with all power, according to His glorious might, for the attaining of all steadfastness and patience;"

For Further Study "Walk" is such an interesting and important study. Find more passages that describe our walk.

Another old hymn that can help us in our walk is Stepping in the Light.

HYMN

Stepping in the Light E.Hewitt (1890) Public Domain

Trying to walk in the steps of the Savior,
Trying to follow our Savior and King;
Shaping our lives by His blessed example,
Happy, how happy, the songs that we bring.

Refrain: How beautiful to walk in the steps of the Savior,
Stepping in the light, stepping in the light,
How beautiful to walk in the steps of the Savior,
Led in paths of light.

Pressing more closely to Him Who is leading,
When we are tempted to turn from the way;
Trusting the arm that is strong to defend us,
Happy, how happy, our praises each day. Refrain.

Trying to walk in the steps of the Savior,
Upward, still upward, we follow our Guide;
When we shall see Him, "the King in His beauty,"
Happy, how happy, our place at His side.

BE WISE

"Oh, the depth of the riches both of the wisdom and knowledge of
God." Romans 11:33

HOW JESUS IS WISE:

We might say that it is not wise to go outside in the rain,
but this is man's wisdom, not Bible wisdom. We will define Bible
wisdom as "the ability to discern what is morally true or right and
practice it."

"Oh, the depth of the riches both of the wisdom and
knowledge of God! How unsearchable are His judgments and
unfathomable His ways!" (Romans 11:33). The apostle Paul wrote
this exclamation after he had presented a complicated discussion of
the Jews' and Gentiles' rejection of God. He summed up by
declaring, in essence, that even though both had lived in
disobedience, God will show mercy in response to their faith in
Christ. Then Paul delivers this beautiful thought, structured much
like a psalm, expressing profound wonder over God's wisdom.
Surely, we have experienced this amazement over the infinite
wisdom and knowledge of God.

On two occasions in His childhood, it was said that Jesus
was increasing in wisdom: once when he was very young, right after
his return to Nazareth from Egypt, and again after the visit to the
temple at twelve years of age (Luke 2:40, 52). The wisdom of Jesus
astonished those of Nazareth, his hometown. "They were
astonished, and said, 'Where did this man get this wisdom and these
miraculous powers?'" (Matthew 13:54). Another time, the officers
of the temple said, "Never has a man spoken the way this man
speaks." (John 6:46). God's wisdom is not like man's. Jesus'
teaching was different. Read Matthew 5-7, the Sermon on the

Mount. Jesus' teaching was revolutionary because it was God's wisdom, not man's.

Jesus did not come as a great scholar of the elite Jewish schools to appeal to the haughtiness of the worldly wise, but as a humble servant, teaching a humble gospel to a humble people. Paul spoke about this in 1 Corinthians 1: 26-27, "For consider your calling, brethren, that there were not many wise according to the flesh, not many mighty, not many noble; [27]but God has chosen the foolish things of the world to shame the wise." He also says in Colossians 2:3 that in Christ "are hidden all the treasures of wisdom and knowledge." Imagine unearthing a great treasure chest and opening it to find great treasures of wisdom and knowledge. That is the idea here of the wisdom that can be found in Christ. Proverbs 8:11 says that wisdom is better than jewels, "and all desirable things cannot compare with her." Job declared, "With Him are wisdom and might; To Him belong counsel and understanding" (Job 12:13).

Paul closes his powerful letter to the Romans with a great psalm of praise. He says, "To Him who is able to establish you according to my gospel and the preaching of Jesus Christ, according to the revelation of the mystery which has been kept secret for long ages past, [26]but now is manifested, and by the Scriptures of the prophets, according to the commandment of the eternal God, has been made known to all the nations, leading to obedience of faith; [27]to the only wise God, through Jesus Christ, be the glory forever. Amen" (Romans 16:25-27). We may want to read this very complicated psalm of praise over and over and break it into its parts to fully comprehend it.

Let us also praise the "only wise God through Christ Jesus." To Him be the glory!

HOW WE CAN BE WISE:

We must begin our search for wisdom with this thought: there can be no wisdom apart from God's word. All of our wisdom comes from Him and can only be found in Him. "My son, if you receive my words, And treasure my commandments within you, Make your ear attentive to wisdom, Incline your heart to understanding; For if you cry for discernment, Lift your voice for understanding; If you seek her as silver And search for her as for hidden treasures; Then you will discern the fear of the LORD And discover the knowledge of God. For the LORD gives wisdom; From His mouth come knowledge and understanding" (Proverbs 2:1-6).

We do not have a quick-fix strategy for obtaining God's wisdom. Here are three ways the scriptures tell us to obtain wisdom:

1. We must desire it with all our heart. As Solomon says, we must "seek her as silver and search for her as for hidden treasure" (Proverbs 2:4). Do we have this passionate longing for wisdom?

2. As James tell us, "If any of you lacks wisdom, let him ask of God, who gives to all generously and without reproach, and it will be given to him" (James 1:5). Do we make it a part of our daily prayers to ask God for wisdom, especially in specific areas where we need it?

3. God's word gives wisdom. Paul said to Timothy, "And that from childhood you have known the sacred writings which are able to give you the wisdom that leads to salvation through faith which is in Christ Jesus" (2 Timothy 3:15).

Wise living starts with fearing the Lord. "The fear of the LORD is the beginning of wisdom, and the knowledge of the Holy One is understanding" (Proverbs 9:10). Fearing the Lord is recognizing that He is the source of all wisdom and willingly submitting to Him and His rule. Without this, there is no wisdom.

198

Wise living grows by daily receiving God's word. "The law of the LORD is perfect, restoring the soul; The testimony of the LORD is sure, making wise the simple" (Psalm 19:7). Only the Bible can show us the mind of God where all wisdom resides.

Wise living matures when we reject our own wisdom for God's. In Jeremiah 9:23a, 24, the Lord says, "Let not a wise man boast of his wisdom... but let him who boasts boast of this, that he understands and knows Me, that I am the LORD who exercises lovingkindness, justice and righteousness on earth; for I delight in these things." Specifically, the teaching is about humbly accepting God over self. So the question is, do we humbly accept that God's way is the best?

Solomon is our great example of seeking wisdom. When God promised him whatever he asked, Solomon answered in such humility, "Now, O LORD my God, You have made Your servant king in place of my father David, yet I am but a little child; I do not know how to go out or come in. ⁸Your servant is in the midst of Your people which You have chosen, a great people who are too many to be numbered or counted. ⁹So give Your servant an understanding heart to judge Your people to discern between good and evil. For who is able to judge this great people of Yours?" (1 Kings 3:7-9). God was pleased that Solomon had asked for this thing. If it pleased God that Solomon asked for wisdom, it will please Him if we do as well.

For Further Study There is so much instruction on wisdom in the scriptures. Do a word search to find more passages. What could be more valuable to study? We found Job 28. It is a great hidden wisdom gem. What will you find?

WORK

"Be steadfast, immovable, always abounding in the work of the
Lord, knowing that your toil is not in vain in the Lord."
I Corinthians 15:58

HOW JESUS WORKED:

Even Jesus had work to do. He could have lived a leisurely
life, constantly served by others. But even at twelve years old, He
seemed to realize that He had work to do for the Father.
Remember when He told His mother, "Did you not know that I
must be about My Father's business?" (Luke 2:49b NKJV)?

In Isaiah 53:11 it was prophesied that Jesus would be a
Servant, and Matthew 20:28 confirms it: "Just as the Son of
Man did not come to be served, but to serve, and to give His life a
ransom for many." Philippians 2:7: "But He emptied Himself,
taking the form of a bond-servant, and being made in the likeness
of men." What might we do if we had unlimited power and
resources? What did Jesus do? He could have been a great earthly
ruler that brought everyone to their knees before Him, but He
chose to be a servant instead. As He said, "But I am among you as
the one who serves" (Luke 22:27).

Jesus recognized the urgency of His work. In John 9:4, he
uses day and night as metaphors to describe this urgency. "We must
work the works of Him who sent Me as long as it is day; night is
coming when no one can work." In a time without strong artificial
lighting, day was the time to work, but it is a limited time. "Day"
refers to the time left for Jesus to serve God here, and "night" to
the rapidly approaching time when His work would end. It is a
lesson for us as well. Our time on earth is limited.

Jesus described His work in Luke 19:10, choosing words filled with great victory for us. He said, "For the Son of Man has come to seek and to save that which was lost." Without Jesus' work, we would still be lost. For me, the Almighty Creator, God's Son, left heaven and became man; for me, He resisted all temptation, living a perfect life; for me, He was arrested, tortured, and hung on a cross; for me, He took my sin upon Himself; for me, He returned from the dead, and now by His great work, I am saved. It was Jesus' work to do.

HOW WE MUST WORK:

For many people, "work" is not a word that brings joy, and yet, work was given to us by God, all the way back in the Garden of Eden. Genesis 2:15 says, "Then the Lord God took the man and put him into the garden of Eden to cultivate it and keep it." We should not get the image of Adam lounging around in the garden; his work was to cultivate and keep it. Man worked from the beginning, and then when he sinned, his work intensified (Genesis 3:17-19). We sometimes think that Adam's punishment was that he had to begin to work, but rather, it was that his work was made harder.

The apostle Paul deals with physical work in 2 Thessalonians 3, summing it up with, "If anyone is not willing to work, then he is not to eat, either. ¹¹For we hear that some among you are leading an undisciplined life, doing no work at all, but acting like busybodies. ¹²Now such persons we command and exhort in the Lord Jesus Christ to work in quiet fashion and eat their own bread" (Verses 10-12). Several proverbs address those who are too lazy to work. Proverbs 10:4-5 says, "Poor is he who works with a negligent hand, But the hand of the diligent makes rich. He who gathers in summer is a son who acts wisely, But he who sleeps in harvest is a son who acts shamefully." Twelve proverbs condemn the lazy "sluggard."

If physical work is a challenge for us, we need to focus on this: "Whatever you do, do your work heartily, as for the Lord rather than for men, [24] knowing that from the Lord you will receive the reward of the inheritance. It is the Lord Christ whom you serve" (Colossians 3:23-24). Even though this instruction is to bondservants, it can be generalized to all. Ask God for joy in work. Thank Him that we can work to provide for our families' needs; thank Him for the clothes we must launder, for the food as we cook for our family, and for our homes as we clean.

God also expects spiritual works of righteousness of all Christians. Works alone without the grace of God will not save us. Yet the scriptures point out clearly that there is work we must do to please Him.

What if the president of the United States asked us to come work in the White House. (Think of the position, not the person). We would perhaps consider that a great honor. Now think of our Master in the kingdom of heaven. What a great privilege to work for Him. We have sung the old hymn, *I Want to be a Worker for the Lord* (I. Baltzell) so much that we may take the words for granted. Let us set our hearts to find joy in our work for the Lord.

Paul urges the young preacher Timothy to view himself as a worker diligently seeking to please his Master. "Be diligent to present yourself approved to God as a workman who does not need to be ashamed, accurately handling the word of truth" (2 Timothy 2:15). Earlier in the chapter, he had compared Timothy to a soldier, athlete, farmer, and now workman. He will not need to be ashamed of his work if he accurately handles the word of truth.

Compensation for our work is one of the key elements that we use to judge a job. What are the benefits of the job, including how much it pays? Working for the Lord brings great compensation. "Therefore, my beloved brethren, be steadfast, immovable, always abounding in the work of the Lord, knowing that your toil is not in vain in the Lord" (1 Corinthians 15:58).

For Further Study: Look at 1 Thessalonians 1:3. Would Paul say that of us? Faith produces work. Love produces labor. Hope produces endurance. Think of work that you can do. How can we be motivated to do our physical work with more joy?

HYMN

To the Work (Fanny Crosby)

To the work! to the work! we are servants of God,
Let us follow the path that our Master has trod;
With the balm of His counsel our strength to renew,
Let us do with our might what our hands find to do.

Refrain: Toiling on, toiling on, Toiling on, toiling on:
Let us hope, let us watch, And labor till the Master comes.

To the work! to the work! let the hungry be fed;
To the fountain of life let the weary be led;
In the cross and its banner our glory shall be,
While we herald the tidings, "Salvation is free!" [Refrain]

To the work! to the work! in the strength of the Lord,
And a robe and a crown shall our labor reward;
When the home of the faithful our dwelling shall be,
And we shout with the ransomed, "Salvation is free!" [Refrain]

WORTHY

"Only conduct yourselves in a manner worthy of the gospel of Christ." Phillipians 1:27

HOW JESUS IS WORTHY:

The word "worth" has an interesting meaning. It originally meant balancing the scales or having the weight of another thing of like value. To determine worth, an object, such as gold, would be put on one side of the scales, and the thing to be appraised would be placed on the other side. That would determine its worth. Therefore, "worthy" can be defined as having adequate worth relative to a standard, demand or expectation. Think of the worthy woman in Proverbs 31:10. Her worth is "far above jewels."

God is worthy. In Revelation 4:10-11, John affords us a view of the glorious heavenly throne room. He writes, "the twenty-four elders will fall down before Him who sits on the throne, and will worship Him who lives forever and ever, and will cast their crowns before the throne, saying, [11] 'Worthy are You, our Lord and our God, to receive glory and honor and power; for You created all things, and because of Your will they existed, and were created.'" Think of the weight if we put God's accomplishments on one side of the scales. We could never pour out adequate glory, honor, and praise to balance the scales of their worth. He is worthy of all we could give and much, much more.

Jesus is worthy. In Revelation 5:6-9 John continues the scene in the throne room. As you read, focus especially on the Lamb of God. "And I saw between the throne (with the four living creatures) and the elders a Lamb standing, as if slain, having seven horns and seven eyes, which are the seven Spirits of God, sent out into all the earth. [7] And He came and took the book out of the right hand of Him who sat on the throne. [8] When He had taken the book, the four living creatures and the twenty-four elders fell down before the Lamb, each one holding a harp and golden bowls full of incense, which are the prayers of the saints. [9] And they sang a new song, saying, 'Worthy are You to take the book and to break its seals; for You were slain, and purchased for God with Your blood men from every tribe and tongue and people and nation.'"

Jesus as the sacrifice, the slain Lamb made Him worthy to take the scroll from God and open it. This scroll seems to symbolize the judgment of God on sin and wickedness, as revealed later by the opening of the seals in chapters 6-8. The Lamb was the only one found worthy to open it.

In verses 11-14, John further describes what he sees. "Then I looked, and I heard the voice of many angels around the throne and the living creatures and the elders; and the number of them was myriads of myriads, and thousands of thousands, [12] saying with a loud voice, 'Worthy is the Lamb that was slain to receive power and riches and wisdom and might and honor and glory and blessing.' And every created thing which is in heaven and on the earth and under the earth and on the sea, and all things in them, I heard saying, 'To Him who sits on the throne, and to the Lamb, be blessing and honor and glory and dominion forever and ever.' [14] And the four living creatures kept saying, 'Amen.' And the elders fell down and worshiped." How privileged we are to read about this glorious scene. It thrills our hearts to think that one day, we could be among those allowed in that throng, praising Him forever who is worthy to be praised.

HOW WE CAN BE WORTHY:

Our natural response is, "Oh, no, I could never be worthy." And yes, that is true. Without the blood of Jesus, we could never be worthy of God's rich blessings that He pours on us. We were sinners and estranged from God when He sent His Son to save us. On our side of the balance scale were our sins, which made us worthy of death. "For the wages of sin is death, but the free gift of God is eternal life in Christ Jesus our Lord" (Romans 6:23). There is nothing that we could ever do that makes us worthy of the death of Christ, but because of our faith in Jesus, He lifts all those sins off the scale and deems us worthy of eternal life.

We are exhorted to walk worthy of our calling (Ephesians 4:1), worthy of the gospel (Philippians 1:27), worthy of the Lord (Colossians 1:10), worthy of God (1 Thessalonians 2:12), and worthy of the kingdom (2 Thessalonians 1:5). How can we possibly accomplish these?

We think of the word worthy as meaning "deserving," and that is sometimes its meaning. Certainly, both God and Jesus are deserving of all our praise and submission. But worthy frequently means "suitable", or "that which is appropriate." Consider Ephesians 4:1: "Walk in a manner worthy of the calling with which you have been called." We accomplish this when our daily living is suitable for our esteemed position as a child of God and fellow heir with Jesus Christ. Our practical living matches our spiritual position. Even then, we do not merit, deserve, or earn the Lord, His calling, and His kingdom, and this is not the meaning of the word "worthy" here. In the words of Jesus: "So you too, when you do all the things which are commanded you, say, 'We are unworthy slaves; we have done only that which we ought to have done'" (Luke 17:10).

Philippians 1:27: "Only conduct yourselves in a manner worthy of the gospel of Christ." Colossians 1:10: "So that you will walk in a manner worthy of the Lord." 1 Thessalonians 2:12: "So that you would walk in a manner worthy of the God who calls you into His own kingdom and glory." All of these are exhortations for a godly life. Walking worthy of our calling is walking moment-by-moment in intimate fellowship with Him in obedience, like a trusting child with his loving father. When we live like this, we are suitable for the gospel and walking worthy.

In 2 Thessalonians 1:5, Paul praises their perseverance in persecution: "This is a plain indication of God's righteous judgment so that you will be considered worthy of the kingdom of God, for which indeed you are suffering." Paul is not saying that enduring trials with faith earns them a place in God's kingdom, but that their faith and obedience indicate their suitableness for the kingdom. 2 Thessalonians 1:11 likewise says: To this end also we pray for you always, that our God will count you worthy of your calling and fulfill every desire for goodness and the work of faith with power."

For Further Study How great it is to serve a God who is deserving of all our praise and submission. Contemplating his goodness, love, and justice inspires our praise. Many of our hymns focus on the worthiness of the Lord. Find several of these hymns and worship with them. Do a word search for worthy. It may surprise you how many times in scripture the word is used. It makes for a good study. As you do your word search, write down your questions and observations. Look at each context. When does "worthy" mean deserving, and when does it mean suitable?

AFTER THE STUDY

By God's grace and mercy, Cynthia and I have made over a three years-long study creating these lessons. As we close, let us think of the hymn Take My Life and Let It Be, F. Havergal (1874). It says,

> Take my life and let it be
> Consecrated, Lord, to Thee.
> Take my moments and my days,
> Let them flow in endless praise.

Is this not our goal? That our life be dedicated to the Lord and our days flowing with endless praise? Another verse of the song says,

> Take my love, my Lord, I pour
> At Thy feet its treasure store.
> Take myself and I will be
> Ever, only, all for Thee.

Pouring our love out at Jesus' feet is an act of worship. Let us strive to be ever only, all for Him.

As we close this study, let God's words encourage us to continue on to be more and more like Jesus.

1 John 2:6 "The one who says he abides in Him ought himself to walk in the same manner as He walked."

God bless you in your walk.

Made in the USA
Columbia, SC
01 July 2024

37778918R00117